Dead Jew Walking

Praise for Dead Jew Walking

"*Hugh Nemets is an amazing guy with an astonishing tale to tell.* Dead Jew Walking *is his story; one he had to write, and one that has to be read by all who struggle to 'pass from death to life' in this shared journey on earth. Like Hugh, I am a Jewish believer in Yeshua-Jesus and a fellow traveler along many of these same challenging paths. But you don't have to be Jewish to relate to this honest, heartfelt and passionate account of one man's pilgrimage through the darkness of this world into the peace and redemption of the 'Light of the World!'*

"*Many are sure to be deeply touched by Hugh's story, profoundly blessed by his courage to share it, and greatly inspired to continue on with joy and hope, whatever road they are 'walking!'*"

~ Marty Goetz, Messianic Musician

"*A captivating read about God's mercy and love in pursuit of one man's heart. This riveting tale of God's faithfulness in the face of near death and destruction will surely challenge and encourage all who pick up this book!*"

~ Debbie and Michael W. Smith, Singer/Songwriter

"*Few books I've read reveal more of a person's brokenness than* Dead Jew Walking *by Hugh Nemets. That may sound negative; it's anything but, for it's in that fragile place of weakness that God is made strong. And surely, this book reveals the strength and faithfulness of God.*

"*Hugh has a compelling way of drawing the reader into what appears to be a dead-end story, with no redeeming conclusion. Yet, each time, we see the hand of God, bringing His grace and mercy and doing miraculous things.*

"*A great book (with a seriously great title) but with an even more powerful message. God not only loves us, He has the power to change us, heal us, and give us a future and a hope.* Dead Jew Walking *is a must-read for anyone needing to experience the God of hope.*"

~ Chris DuPré, Pastor, Speaker, and Author of *The Wild Love of God*

"*This is a story about an ordinary man who encounters an extraordinary God. Hugh Nemets's story will encourage you and give you hope that God will never leave you nor forsake you. No matter how dire your circumstances, He will show you that He is faithful.*"

~ Jeff Dollar, Senior Pastor, Grace Center Church
Franklin, Tennessee

DEAD JEW WALKING

A Jewish Man's Journey from Death to Life

Hugh Nemets

Dead Jew Walking: A Jewish Man's Journey from Death to Life

Copyright © 2016 by Hugh Nemets

ALL RIGHTS RESERVED. Any unauthorized reprint or use of this material is prohibited.

No part of this book whether art or text may be reproduced or transmitted in any form or by any means, electronic or mechanical, including photocopying, recording, or by any information storage and retrieval system without express written permission from the author except in the case of brief quotations embodied in critical articles and reviews. For more information, contact 4319 Publishing, publisher@deadjewwalking.com.

All Scripture quotations, unless otherwise indicated, are taken from *The New King James Version*.

Copyright © 1979, 1980, 1982, Thomas Nelson, Inc. Some Scripture quotations marked (AMP) are taken from *The Amplified® Bible*. Copyright © 1954, 1958, 1962, 1964, 1965, 1987 by The Lockman Foundation. Used by permission. (www.Lockman.org) Scripture quotations marked (CJB) are taken from *The Complete Jewish Bible* copyright © 1998 by David H. Stern. All rights reserved.

ISBN Print: 978-0-9968987-0-6

ISBN eBook: 978-0-9968987-1-3

ISBN ePDF: 978-0-9968987-2-0

Library of Congress Control Number: 2015955051

1. Atheism 2. Christianity/Salvation 3. Heavenly vison 4. Redemption 5. Pornography addictions 6. Divorce 7. Backsliding 8. Drugs/Alcohol 9. Abortion 10. Suicide 11. Dysfunctional family 12. Survival

I. Nemets, Hugh II. Dead Jew Walking: A Jewish Man's Journey from Death to Life

This publication is designed to provide accurate and authoritative information in regard to the subject matter covered. It is sold with the understanding that neither the author nor the publisher is engaged in rendering any type of professional services. If expert assistance is required, the services of a competent professional should be sought.

Dead Jew Walking may be purchased at special quantity discounts. Resale opportunities are available for sales promotions, corporate programs, gifts, fund raising, book clubs, or educational purposes for churches, congregations, schools and universities. For more information, visit www.deadjewwalking.com/resellers.

Cover design and layout: Bart Elliott, BAE Productions www.baeproductions.com

Interior design and layout: Lynne Hopwood

Publishing Consultant: Mel Cohen, Inspired Authors Press, LLC www.inspiredauthorspress.com

Editor: Anne Severance

Printed in the United States of America

Publisher: 4319 Publishing

To have Hugh Nemets speak at your next event, live or by videoconferencing, write to author@deadjewwalking.com for booking information and details.

Dedication

To my Savior, Lord, and Master, Yeshua, my Messiah

Your love is furious and vast, and You always seek to redeem and restore, especially in our darkest days, at the midnight hours. Thank You, Yeshua, for taking all my punishment, always standing as my Advocate, and never leaving or forsaking me. You gladly paid the highest price to buy back a soul that I thought was worthless—my own—and You are preparing a mansion for me in Your eternal neighborhood. You are truly my Light and my Salvation, my everything.

Contents

Foreword 9
Acknowledgments 11
Introduction 13
Chapter 1 Nine Millimeters from Death 17
Chapter 2 Bitter Roots 23
Chapter 3 College, Career, and "Calamity Jane" 33
Chapter 4 Twice Born 39
Chapter 5 Matchmaker, Matchmaker 49
Chapter 6 The Chosen 57
Chapter 7 Yeridah: Back in America 75
Chapter 8 Mid-life Madness 89
Chapter 9 The Awakening 95
Chapter 10 Stricken 107
Chapter 11 This Year in Jerusalem 123
Appendix 131

Foreword

What a blessing to read Hugh Nemets's *Dead Jew Walking!*

Hugh is a man of character, a gentle, passionate man of God. I wept my way through his well-crafted account of God's continual pursuit of him, from his days as an insecure and often angry Jewish atheist to the transformation that came immediately when he accepted his Messiah; then through the insidious complacency that can engulf us, to the man God has made him to be today.

I have only known Hugh as a godly man who loves Lisa and his children well, and who is well loved by them and by a host of other believers who meet regularly together for worship and prayer. His account of life before Yeshua/Jesus and the transformation that immediately followed is a powerful testimony to the goodness of God and of God's present-day work to call Jewish people to Himself. That part of Hugh's life reminds me of Francis Thompson's poem, "The Hound of Heaven":

> *I fled him down the days and down the years. . . .*
> *I fled him down the labyrinthine ways of my own mind.*

Hugh had no intention of receiving Yeshua until one night when he had come to the end of himself. The suffering Hugh has experienced in recent years is beyond our ability to comprehend. However, the apostle Paul calls suffering God's way of producing character. "We rejoice in our suffering, because we know that suffering produces perseverance, and perseverance character" (Romans 5:3). That, too, has been a part of Hugh and Lisa's lives. Both have become gentle, compassionate, kind and loving disciples of Yeshua. You will appreciate the account of their pilgrimage.

~ Don Finto

"Equipping God's people with His heart and purpose for Israel and the nations. As a follower of Yeshua, I am called to be a Holy Spirit-led, Godly husband, father, grandfather, to my own family, extended family and others, and a prophetic apostolic voice to the people of God, especially those called to leadership, to help raise up and empower the next generations, challenging them through who I am, what I say, and what I write - to be wholeheartedly devoted to the Lord all the days of their lives, to embrace God's prophetic call for Israel and the Jewish people, and thus the Israel key that unlocks world revival, in preparation for the return of the King!"

Acknowledgments

To Lisa: You are my forever bride, soul mate, and life partner on this wild ride; you have never stopped believing in me. We have been through so much together: for richer and poorer, in sickness and in health. You have encouraged me, chided me, pushed me, loved me and stood with me from the very beginning. You have always been my greatest fan and have never doubted me. Without your inspiration, this book would never have been written. Lisa, you will always be the "cream in my coffee" and the love of my life. You are a wife of noble character, an *eschet chayil*. You complete me.

To my beautiful daughters: Lauren, Peri, and Elli, wonderful son-in-law Joe, and my incredible granddaughters, Sophia, Audrey, and Grace. I love you all very much and I'm blessed to have you in my life.

To my editor, Anne Severance: Thank you for helping me to "see the forest through the trees." Your wonderful encouragement, editing skills, and insight enabled this book to finally come to fruition! You have become more than my editor; thanks for allowing me to call you "Mom"!

"Papa" Don Finto: Thank you for your great encouragement and support for this project. I am greatly inspired by you. You are a true reflection of Yeshua.

To my Caleb family: Thank you for your ongoing prayers and support. I am honored to be associated with a group of forerunners and leaders who live their lives with such purity, humility, and power.

Bart Elliott: Your friendship, prayers and skill sets have blessed me beyond words. Thank you for always being available and a friend who is closer than a brother!

Michael Birkland: Your creative gifts are amazing! Thank you for using them to pour into making this project all it could be. You are a huge blessing!

Shawna Splawn: I am grateful for your friendship, as well as your input and editing help, and your prayers in the early formative stages of this work.

Dr. Rick Bennett: Thank you for providing medical insight regarding my illnesses for this work. You have been a great blessing and advocate to me over the years; it is an honor to call you friend.

Harriett Susinno: You spent many hours, rearranged your schedule, helped stir the creative flow when I got mired down. You showed me how to reach deep down and plumb the depths of my mind and soul. I am grateful to you for believing in me. Thank you for your support, prayers, and persistence.

Introduction

"What do I have to share?"

I used to think I had nothing to share, even when many people who read my devotional blog posts told me that I should write a book. I have always struggled with discouragement and have been plagued at times with feelings of self-doubt and inadequacy. I wondered why anyone would be interested in the trials, the testing, and the testimony of my life. I questioned my capabilities and considered myself less than ordinary. Perhaps you have dealt with this yourself. Don't we all struggle from time to time with fear, failure, and discouragement, feeling that we lack significance?

The Lord, in His amazing grace, allowed me a glimpse of eternity—of heaven itself and its magnificence—which was far beyond my imagination. He showed me marvelous things He has prepared for all His children, and He gave me a message to deliver to you. Many of us have no idea how very special we are to our Abba. He uniquely gifts each of us so that our lives can bring glory to Him, our awesome Creator. The Lord, tender in His lovingkindness, gave me instructions to write down this revelation of how He sees us.

You may be, like I was, among the walking dead and not even know it. Busy with many different activities, caught up in the rat race, with little thought of the future. You also, like I at one time, may believe you are invincible and that the "fun" must end in order to accept Yeshua (whose Hebrew name actually means "salvation"; the Gentiles call Him Jesus) as Lord. You may have unanswered questions or a variety of delusions separating you from the Father God who loves you and sent His only begotten Son to die in your place. You may be living your life as if you're the one in control, at least until something happens that suddenly changes everything. That's what happened to me. So I wrote this for you.

Writing a book had never crossed my mind. But after being in the presence of God, I found my thoughts echoing the words of King David:

> *My heart is overflowing with a good theme;*
> *I recite my composition concerning the King;*
> *My tongue is the pen of a ready writer."*

~ Psalm 45:1

I didn't know it then, but the experience awaiting me would forever change me. For I have seen the Lord and He truly is high and lifted up.

Now I understand the Scripture that reads:

> *Eye has not seen, nor ear heard,*
> *Nor have entered into the heart of man*
> *These things God has prepared*
> *for those who love Him.*

~1 Corinthians 2:9

The Lord chose to reveal to me, as His son and co-heir with Yeshua/Jesus, a glimpse of what is in store when I finally go to live in my heavenly mansion for eternity.

I look forward to the day when I will return to stay in my Father's house forever.

I'm homesick.

This is my story.

- 1 -

Nine Millimeters from Death

Stay sober, stay alert!
Your enemy, the Adversary
stalks about like a roaring lion looking
for someone to devour.
~ 1 Peter 5:8 (CJB)

SWAT teams and military units have a tactical weapon—a type of battering ram affectionately nicknamed "the key to the city." This heavy steel tool will quickly and efficiently bash in nearly any door. By the same token, if we crack open a door in our lives while Satan is crouching there, he will use his own version of a battering ram to cave it in. It is more devastating than any of the SWAT teams' high-tech weaponry; it's more like a WMD, a weapon of mass destruction.

There is an old saying: "If you give 'em an inch, they'll take a mile." An inch given to the devil can set us on a dangerous journey that can take us a mile, many miles, light years from home. He is a deceiver and a destroyer. That sweet taste of sin quickly turns into a bitter pill of poison. In other words, the devil is a liar!

In May 2010, I was a mess, engulfed in the throes of private despair during a disastrous period of backsliding, I was drinking too much, addicted to pornography, and verbally abusive to my wife and children. Lisa desperately sought marriage counseling since living with me had become unbearable. Twisted and obsessed by porn, I had broken my holy marriage covenant by bringing that filth into our bedroom. It grieved her terribly, and she saw it for what it was—adultery and idolatry. Our marriage was disintegrating rapidly.

I grabbed hold of Romans (5:20) that reads:

When sin abounds, grace abounds all the more.

I misinterpreted and manipulated this word to serve my purposes. I wanted to have it all my way, but I wanted absolution without repentance. I wanted God to cover it. I wanted a license to sin, thinking I could "pull the wool over" His eyes.

I was dead wrong.

Temporary Problem ... Permanent Solution

The Billy Graham Evangelistic Association states that over 30,000 Americans commit suicide every year, while 750,000 people *attempt* to take their own lives. Suicide has been described as a "permanent solution to a temporary problem."

Yet I almost opted in favor of that "permanent solution." One evening, as I headed home, I found myself passing my normal turn, driving aimlessly as dark thoughts gathered in my mind like storm clouds. I decided to make my way over to the wide-open parking lot of our nearby mall. I pulled up in a secluded area and cut the engine.

As I sat there for a while, tears streaming down my face, I could only see one way out of the mess I felt totally responsible for. Slowly and deliberately, I opened the glove compartment of the car and removed my favorite 9mm pistol—a Heckler Koch P2000SK. A hollow-point bullet waited in the chamber, ready to fire. I handled the weapon, shifting it from one hand to the other. I noticed the perfect balance of the gun and the feel of the grip. As I ran my fingers over its cold, steely contours, I was deep in thought. Although I had acquired this pistol purely for self-defense, I was now eyeing it as an instrument of self-destruction.

I was tired, confused, and totally spent. How could this happen, I wondered. I had been so careful. We had done what we thought were the "right" things financially. Yet here we were, being sued for hundreds of thousands of dollars for a failed business venture. Our savings, something I had placed my trust in, had been stripped from us. Any hope of an early retirement—dashed. My marriage was in shambles.

The Ultimate Disgrace

But the deepest cut of all—the one that penetrated to the very core of my being—was the look on the innocent face of my beloved middle daughter when she discovered the disgusting images on my computer.

"What are these pictures, Daddy?" Peri asked, turning that trusting face up to me, waiting for my answer.

There was no defense.

As a father, it was my hope that I would always be a shining example of "a good man"—a man my children could look up to, a man whose integrity was without question. Among these attributes would be my faithful love for my wife—their mother—with my eyes for her only. My porn habit dashed that hope. My secret life had been discovered.

The look of disappointment on my child's face as I tried, unsuccessfully, to lie my way out was something I'll never forget. I feared that she would never again be able to look up to me as her dad, and that knowledge was unbearable.

Nothing in my life was working out like I had thought it would. Seeing no way out, I just wanted it all to be over. I closed my eyes and leaned back against the headrest, gripping the weapon. My thoughts drifted to events of the past....

Baby Believer

Twenty years after a radical conversion, here I was, gripping a loaded pistol and thinking of ending it all. I might have been born again, but I was still a baby believer. In those two decades since coming to belief in Yeshua, I was plagued with self-consciousness, fearing how I might appear to others. So I remained under the radar, invisible and silent. My walk with God was more of a slow crawl.

As I sat in the mall parking lot, I was having a conversation with the grand accuser. Satan might be invisible, but his presence was almost palpable in my car that day. He hissed in my ear all the reasons why I should put the muzzle of that pistol to my head and pull the trigger. He reminded me of every single one of my failures: I was a lousy husband, lousy father, lousy friend, lousy employee, terrible decision-maker, and a poor excuse for a believer. Furthermore, he told me I was a miserable hypocrite, and with my substantial life insurance policies, would be worth more to Lisa and the kids dead than alive.

Just think...all the pain, suffering, and striving will finally be over, he whispered. *All you have to do is put the gun to your temple and squeeze that hair trigger....*

He was so *smooth*, so persuasive, and his argument made so much sense. It was tempting. . . . The only thing that kept me from killing myself was the legacy of death that would hang over my family.

When I decided not to pull the trigger, he changed his tactics, taunting and berating me into finishing the job. *See?! You're such a coward and screw-up, you can't even do this one last thing right! You're pitiful!*

I slowly de-cocked and holstered the pistol, and drove home with a heavy heart. Yeah, for once he'd told the truth. I was nothing but a coward. Unbeknownst to me, Lisa had been pouring out her heart to God in long hours of travailing prayer. I later learned that she had been interceding for me for months to repent and be restored. But even she had no idea of the depths of depravity to which I had sunk.

It was time to do some drastic soul-searching, some intense inner scrutiny. What had brought me to this moment of hopelessness? After over two decades of being snatched from the clutches of the Grim Reaper on plenty of occasions—not to mention my spiritual salvation, securing my eternal destiny in heaven—why was I now courting death?

To answer that question, I must go back to the beginning, trace the steps of a Jew who should have been dead, but is still walking on God's green earth. . . .

-2-

Bitter Roots

*Fathers (and mothers), don't irritate your children
and make them resentful,
or they will become discouraged.*
~ Colossians 3:21 (CJB)

In trying to understand how I arrived at this place of desperation, I must go further back in time, back to my childhood. I am amazed at how little I actually knew about my parents' histories—their strengths, their weaknesses, what made them tick. In my later years, so many questions emerged. I would have loved to have asked them about their life experiences—what had made them into the people they became.

Therefore, much of the information that follows was gleaned from documents and personal stories from other relatives, with only a few anecdotes from my parents themselves.

I knew only that they had met on Miami Beach in the summer of '55 and married in October 1956. My father's first wife, Rose, succumbed to cancer in 1954, after nineteen years of marriage, leaving my dad a widower with two young daughters. I believe Rose was the love of his life, and my mother spent her life trying to fill those shoes. But that's another story....

My Father, Al Nemets

Dad was a workaholic, consumed with his career. Like so many men of his generation, he believed that providing for his family was his most important priority. On the other hand, I always felt that spending time with us—the very family he was devoted to providing the "good life" for—was a distant second. Working long hours, he seemed to prefer the camaraderie of his colleagues and customers, thriving on the hustle of the restaurant business. His work habits were fueled by two things: first and foremost was a desire never to lack again. He had endured terrible deprivation as a boy in Russia—had gone hungry and witnessed persecution as a Jew—and had lived through the Great Depression here in America when his family immigrated. Secondly, I think he wanted to distance himself from my mother's incessant complaints of poor health.

My father had worked his way up from nothing financially, was a well-known Miami Beach restaurateur and was justifiably proud of his achievements. He and his first wife had owned a number of famous eateries including Al's Sandwich Shop on 23rd Street and the Rendezvous, both on Miami Beach, and Al Nemets's Restaurant in Chicago. During most of my childhood and until his retirement in 1978, he was the general manager of two landmark Miami Beach restaurants, the Roney Pub and the Newport Pub. They were among the most popular of their time on the "Beach," with customers willing to wait hours to dine there.

The restaurants' success was a well-known fact, and he prided himself on never taking a day off in seven years. He gave us, his children, everything money could buy, but he rarely gave us the most valuable thing—his time. There were those cherished moments like occasional early-morning trips to the bagel shop on Ocean Drive to pick up piping hot bagels. I can almost still smell the wonderful aroma wafting through his Cadillac as we drove home.

At other times, we had to go to the restaurant if we wanted to see Dad, hoping he would break away long enough to have dinner with us. Those visits were always special, enhanced by the memory of many of his long-time employees. There was Marguerite, the ever-smiling cashier, eyes twinkling from behind her 1950's style cat's-eye glasses; Bernie, the bartender, who was a real comedian and always had a funny joke to tell me; Max, my father's faithful steward, as well as 6'6" Willis and silver-haired Cuban Pete, two of the hearth chefs. These special people were like family to me, and they watched over me with affection as I matured from a boy into a young man.

Dad was not a religious man; I don't remember him ever going to *Erev Shabbat* services at our temple, or observing any Jewish holidays besides Rosh HaShanah, Yom Kippur, and Passover. In a way, I think he *blamed* God and being Jewish for the trouble and hardship he endured in Russia and the anti-Semitism he personally experienced in the United States. My father had told me that, in that era, many establishments had posted signs reading: "No Jews, dogs, or colored people allowed." As a U.S. Navy man, enlisting at the age of thirty-five shortly after the Japanese attacked Pearl Harbor, I believe he had a difficult time believing in a God who would allow six million Jews to perish in the Holocaust—"Hitler's Final Solution."

During his military service, he entrusted the management of the restaurants to Rose. Dad spoke quite a few languages, including German, but after World War II, he despised Germans as well as the Japanese, and apparently never got over the fact that only a few decades before, they had been our mortal enemies.

Although my father had many shortcomings, I loved him. My fondest memory is of him picking me up off the carpet in front of our wooden console, black-and-white Zenith TV, where I would often feign being asleep after watching my favorite show, *Lassie*. In my mind, I can still smell the wonderful scent of his Fabergé cologne as he carried me to my bed. My dad was not ashamed of public displays of affection, and never hesitated blessing me with his hugs and kisses, whether greeting me or saying goodbye. I never quite understood the strange dichotomy in our relationship, though—that he could be generous with his affection and so stingy with his time, which was the thing I most yearned for.

Lung cancer took my father's life on October 22, 1989. He died before I could reach his bedside, as Lisa and I were on a flight home from Israel. I would struggle for years with my anger and bitterness toward him for not being there for me in my younger years, compounded by my disgust with myself for squandering so many opportunities to be with him in his later years. So I, too, wasted time—that precious and irreplaceable commodity.

Dorothy, My Mom

Like my father, Mom shared very little about her past with us. After her death, we pieced together scraps of her childhood from chats with aunts and uncles, and articles from old newspaper clippings.

She was next to the youngest of twelve children, born to immigrant farmer parents, in Browerville, Minnesota. In 1923 her father (my grandfather, Michael) fell through thin ice on a lake and after being pulled from those icy waters, contracted pneumonia and subsequently died at the age of 45, leaving my grandmother to raise their dozen children—ages three to twenty—alone. My mom was only five years old at the time. I can't begin to imagine the impact the loss of her father had on her, but in many ways, I believe my mom's identity and decisions were based on her having an orphan mentality from which she never recovered.

In those days, children were not considered liabilities, but assets; everyone had a job to do on the farm as together they worked to sustain the family. Even my mother and her three-year-old sister, Theresa—nicknamed "Bobbie"—helped feed the chickens and did whatever else they could do to help. But no one sat around idly.

In 1950, she and Bobbie migrated to Florida where my mom married and later divorced her abusive first husband. After the divorce, she and her sister applied for waitressing jobs at my dad's restaurant, and he hired them.

My dad, quite dashing and an elegant dresser, looked a lot like Walt Disney or maybe Errol Flynn, a famous movie star of that day, and my mom fell head over heels in love with him at first sight. They were married for 33 years and three days... and I suspect that not a day went by that he didn't think about Rose.

My sisters and I later uncovered another secret. As we talked about the timeline of certain events, it became apparent that my parents were married after the birth of my brother, and while my mother was pregnant with me. This would have been quite a scandal in those days!

In thinking of my mother, her life impressed me as one of chronic pain and assorted illnesses. I'm not sure if they were real or contrived, but it seemed that she was always sick. I wondered if this was her method of gaining my father's sympathy and attention because of his constant focus on the restaurant—his mistress. Perhaps Mom was just tired, worn out from taking care of four kids all day, or maybe she was taking too many medications. But whatever the reason, she was never really positively involved with my life, and as I matured, I grew to resent it.

I wonder as to why certain images remain fixed in one's memory. One of my memories of Mom is the meal she prepared for my brother and me almost every day for years—a broiled sirloin strip steak, baked potato, and a tossed salad with her homemade Italian vinaigrette dressing. Another is of her beautiful hands and perfectly manicured nails. In spite of the dysfunction she brought into my life, I loved her, even pitied her. But it took years for me to forgive her.

My mom died on New Year's Day, 1996, from congestive heart failure—once again, before I had wrestled down the demon of unforgiveness.

Childhood Lost

I was the youngest of the four Nemets children. My sisters, Jodi and Garen, were nine and ten years older. Because there was half a generation gap between us, we never really knew each other; we were just acquaintances living under the same roof. Both of them got married by the time they were twenty, probably to escape life in our household with my mother (their stepmother), although they, like my brother and I, did adore our father.

Our family never took a vacation together except for a three-day excursion to the Florida Keys once, after my sisters had married and left home. My birthdays were consistently overlooked; I never really had a birthday party as a child. In fact, my eighth birthday was completely ignored by both my parents and my siblings till the end of the day. That summer of 1965, they were preoccupied with the recent move into our Miami Beach home.

They all apologized, but that didn't change the way I felt—insignificant and forgotten.

One would think that what could have been a near-fatal accident would trigger some kind of maternal sympathy. In 1966, when I was nine, there were no bicycle helmets, no knee or elbow pads. I was riding my banana-seat bike with the high handle bars across the Venetian Causeway that slices through the middle of DiLido Island, where we lived near Miami Beach. Suddenly my sneakered right foot slipped off the pedal on the down stroke and somehow jammed into the spokes of the front wheel. The bike flipped upside down and launched me about ten feet into the air. I landed on my head and shoulder in the intersection of the street amidst the flow of traffic. No neck damage. No concussion. And no motherly concern.

In fact, my mother had an interesting way of encouraging us. It was common for her to make deeply wounding comments to my brother and me: "You will never be able to fill your father's shoes," or " You'll never be half the man your father is." These words burned into my psyche like a fiery brand, and to this day I can still hear their scalding echo. Those declarations became the inner voice that defined me. Since I never could live up to those lofty expectations, I took the path of least resistance. Perseverance, the discipline of "stick-to-it-iv-ity," was not developed as a young man. I never learned to push through difficulties or set goals, and settled for the questionable satisfaction of just getting by . . . or escaping into sporting activities and daring adventures.

Close Calls

In 1970, the year of my Bar Mitzvah, there were two scuba diving incidents, either of which could have easily resulted in my drowning. I was young, carefree, and impetuous—a deadly combo. I thought I was invincible. Furthermore, I was not scuba-certified.

The first diving event happened at Belle Isle, near a small bridge on the Venetian Causeway in the waters of Biscayne Bay, just one hundred yards from my friend Casey's houseboat. Casey had taught me the basics, just enough to be dangerous. The waters were murky and the incoming tide rushing into the narrow inlet was threatening to sweep us away. I was weighed down with heavy gear, and since I was not wearing a buoyancy compensation (BC) vest, it took every ounce of energy I could muster to swim upwards and avoid sinking to the bottom. It was a miracle that I was able to make it to a concrete bridge pylon and wait to be rescued.

The second scuba incident happened in the waters near Bimini, a Bahamian island just 48 miles from the coast of Florida, during the Fourth of July weekend, 1970. I was invited to sail to Bimini with my diving pal, Casey, and his family. Not even a nasty sinus infection would deter me, even after the first fiasco.

We were in about twenty-five feet of water when a blood vessel burst in my sinuses, causing a severe nosebleed into my mask. Looking down, I could see quite a lot of blood! I couldn't wash it out because there were sharks in the area and one six-foot-long barracuda that was eyeing us. The current was swift, tugging us away from safety. Casey and I were swimming as hard as we could, but making no headway. Just when I was beginning to panic, a couple in a small skiff realized we were in trouble and rescued us. Angels on assignment? Maybe. But I was still too cocky to admit I needed help, especially from a God I did not believe existed.

Faith of Our Father?

Spiritual matters were never discussed in our home, and because of this, I had only a marginal interest in my Jewish identity and basically no interest in God. This was where my unbelief began to take root. We were members of Temple Beth Shalom, a reform synagogue on Miami Beach. In my opinion now as a believer, the reform movement is nothing more than secular humanism. The Torah was not considered to be the infallible Word of God. I suspect that many Reform Jews cannot truly believe in a God who would allow so many catastrophes—the Inquisition, pogroms in Europe, the Holocaust—so they embrace a personal "god in me." I recall messages from the *bimah* emphasizing the triumph of man and the strength of humanity, rather than man's weaknesses and God's unending love for His chosen people. To me, God was a nebulous theory at best.

I studied at my temple's Hebrew school for three years for my Bar Mitzvah, the ceremonial rite of passage from boyhood to manhood in Judaism. I can tell you that even at that time, I was an atheist. I simply couldn't bring myself to believe in something or someone I could not see. To top it off, no one around me—not a teacher, student, parent nor rabbi—addressed these issues. In my world, and for most Jews I was associated with, Judaism was a cultural and social phenomenon—not a belief system.

My atheistic mindset was strengthened as I studied chemistry, biology, and evolution. It wasn't that I was actively trying to refute God and religion. I simply wasn't thinking about God at all—or anything to do with Him. As a carnally minded young man, I simply wanted to do what I wanted to do. My animus against "religious" people in general and Christians specifically would not come until later, as I began to run out of options and made one wrong life choice after another.

Still, my brother and I were raised as Jews in accordance with my father's faith and wishes, even though my mother had come from a Gentile background. I kept this information to myself—mostly for my own protection. In modern Judaism, a person's Jewish identity is dependent on the mother being Jewish, which is the opposite of biblical Judaism, where the lineage is traced through the father's line. At my temple and in my religious studies, we were warned explicitly about the dangers of religious intermarriage so as not to dilute our Jewish identity, eventually causing assimilation and ultimately, the disappearance of the Jewish people. Because of this, I secretly feared being discovered as religiously "impure" or a "spiritual half-breed," often wondering, *Where do I belong?* I desired to feel wholly Jewish, but the nagging sense of incompleteness haunted me.

In school, I always made very high grades (mostly "A's" with an occasional "B"), and in high school I was invited to join the National Honor Society, but I did not join. Why bother? I perceived that my parents were not interested in my scholastic achievements. Nor did I attend my prom or my graduation. Instead of "taking the walk" with my classmates to the tune of "Pomp and Circumstance," I requested that my diploma be mailed to me.

Neither my mother nor my father ever attended a school function, a parent-teacher conference, a sporting event, or any other scholastic activity. I was well fed and well clothed, but I was not really parented. For example, I had my own "don't ask, don't tell" policy. They had no idea I had been sexually active since I was fourteen, primarily to boost my below-the-gutter level of self-esteem. To feel loved and wanted. To believe, for a few stolen moments, that someone—anyone— desired me.

Would I ever amount to anything, and if so, did anyone care?

-3-

College, Career, and "Calamity Jane"

*So let us not grow weary of doing what is good,
For if we don't give up we will in due time
reap the harvest.*
~ Galatians 6:9 (CJB)

After graduating from high school with a 3.75 GPA, I gladly bade farewell to my childhood home, and off I went to Florida State University (FSU) in Tallahassee. There I enrolled as a pre-med student.

I had applied to and was accepted by three universities: Florida State, University of Florida, and George Washington University. My reason for choosing FSU made no rational sense. It was all about a girl. My summertime girlfriend of four years had been accepted at FSU, but not UF, and I wanted to be with her. Not surprisingly, my parents did not even suggest that I take a closer look at my options. One week after arriving on campus, I broke up with the girl. For a while we continued a stormy on-again, off-again relationship until we broke up for good.

I attended FSU for three and a half years, and during that time I changed my major three times, all the while moving from one disastrous relationship to another. Eventually, I became entangled in a toxic relationship with the girl who would later become my first wife and ultimately, my ex-wife. With this emotional turmoil swirling around me, I lost focus and my grades plummeted. Although my father rarely gave me much direction, I found myself violating the one bit of good advice he had given me: "Steer clear of that girl and end the relationship immediately." Roe v. Wade had become the law of the land in 1973, and there would be two abortions with this girlfriend. I was complicit in these abortions, equally responsible for the deaths of two of my own children.

When I moved back to Miami to escape the ongoing drama, I was only twenty credit hours away from completing a degree. I had intended to change my major yet again to a hotel/hospitality degree when I landed a job at one of the original Tony Roma restaurants in South Miami, quickly working my way up to a management position. The demands of this new career path were so great, the hours so lengthy that the completion of my college degree was postponed indefinitely.

Wedlock/Deadlock

Within a few months of this move, my former FSU girlfriend, whom I had escaped when I left Tallahassee, contacted me. She still loved me, she claimed, and wanted to reconcile and reunite in Miami. Despite our past history and my father's dire warnings, as well as all the "alarms" going off inside my head, I took her back again with open arms. Four months later, she was pregnant again, and so we decided to tie the knot. We were married in a civil ceremony, officiated by my uncle. His fee? One whole pastrami brisket.

My father and mother did make it this time, but they were the only attendees.

A few months later, we welcomed our beautiful baby girl, whom I named Lauren Taylor Nemets, into the world. As we adjusted to our new lives as young parents, I was promoted to a general manager's position at another restaurant chain and relocated to my own store in Ft. Myers, Florida. Following my father's work ethic, I put in 12- to 15-hour days at the restaurant and spent virtually no time with my new family.

Was it any wonder what our next step would be?

* * *

This ill-fated marriage disintegrated in less than two years. I felt totally blindsided and soon found out the real cause of the divorce. My ex-wife had left me for another man—a former neighbor from Miami. They married as soon as our divorce was final and moved from Ft. Meyers back to the Miami area, taking my beloved daughter with them.

The realization that my wife had been having an affair shattered my self-esteem and any concept of trust I thought I had. Shame and failure weighed heavily on me. To maintain my relationship with my toddler daughter, I found myself traveling hundreds of miles every other weekend. I could barely breathe, much less function in my demanding position at the restaurant.

Soon afterwards, unable to perform at my job, I was demoted and transferred to an assistant manager's position in Lakeland, Florida, which meant I was now even farther away from Lauren. I had to arrange our visits weeks in advance and drive 237 miles from Lakeland to South Miami to pick her up. Since we had no family in Miami at that time, I would then have to drive an additional 236 miles to my parents' home in Orlando, and then back the very next day. Each trip I made was like grinding salt into an open wound, and I cried most of the way, coming and going. I found myself driving over a thousand miles in a weekend—just to see my beloved daughter for a few hours.

She was worth every agonizing mile.

* * *

When Lauren was five years old, her mother and the second husband petitioned the court to relocate to Brooklyn, NY. My worst fear had become a reality. I was stunned.

To preoccupy myself and improve my self-esteem, I took up bodybuilding and began to use steroids to build up muscle quickly. One of the well-known possible side effects of steroid use is aggressive behavior, and it manifested strongly in me. My anger and bitterness became fuel for the aggression the steroids caused, and I placed the blame squarely on my ex-wife. The shame of the divorce and the loss of my daughter continued to eat away at me, until the rage building within me reached the combustible point. On two separate occasions, I threatened to murder my ex-wife and her second husband. They took my threats seriously, and rightfully so; I was seriously disturbed.

I shouldn't have been surprised when they filed a complaint with the Metro-Dade Police Department. Soon afterwards, I received a visit from a Miami plain-clothes detective who stopped by to let me know that if anything happened to them, I would be the prime suspect. I *did* have enough sense to take the detective's advice and stop threatening them.

When they moved North, they took with them my precious daughter—and my reason for living. I was just 26 years old and had no idea how to deal with such emotional pain. The separation from my daughter left a gaping hole in my heart, and added yet another layer of emotional scarring.

Descent into Destiny

Eventually I met and fell in love with a wonderful girl, but it didn't take long for that relationship to sour, too. My jealousy and possessiveness were lethal, and after a year and a half of living together, she moved out. Seeing this as yet another failure in my life, I immersed myself in a party lifestyle, complete with heavy drinking, smoking cigarettes, and frequently indulging in my drug of choice, cocaine. I didn't consider myself a full-fledged smoker, since I only smoked when I drank. Who was I kidding? I drank everyday!

As I pursued this empty lifestyle, I eventually contracted sexually transmitted hepatitis B. Today I am amazed that, even during these promiscuous times, the Lord watched over me, and I never contracted any other STD, Hepatitis C or AIDS.

In the spring of 1985, I left the restaurant business for a position in automobile sales, landing a great job at a Ferrari/Audi/Porsche dealership in South Florida. While my work life was successful, my party lifestyle escalated even more in my frantic search for some meaning and happiness. The peace I yearned for was ever elusive.

-4-

Twice Born

> *Therefore if anyone is united with Messiah,
> he is a new creation; the old has passed; look,
> what has come is fresh and new!*
> ~2 Corinthians 5:17 (CJB)

Blaise Pascal describes what he calls "a God-shaped vacuum" that exists within each individual. Many people spend their lives trying to fill this vacuum with whatever they believe will give them identity, meaning, and fulfillment—money, sex, drugs, alcohol, and success topping the list. This was the journey I was on, but as time went by, I grew ever emptier. Outwardly, I was the life of the party, often behaving outrageously, saying and doing things that were very entertaining to my party animal friends. Inside the secret recesses of my aching heart, I was deeply ashamed.

Faith was a concept that I could not comprehend. If I couldn't see it, I didn't believe it. I considered "faith" to be like an opiate, dumbing down and dulling those people I deemed gullible. I embraced the "Looking out for #1" paradigm of my culture. To be honest, I believed I would be dead by the age of forty, so my life didn't matter. No one cared about me. I reasoned that the only logical thing to do was to grab whatever "gusto" I could, while I could.

Christians, I reasoned, were arrogant and exclusive. I remember seeing bumper stickers on cars with the slogan: "Christians aren't perfect, just forgiven." I viewed this segment of society as shallow, ignorant hypocrites, and to validate my opinion, I often quoted the words of other Christian-haters like Karl Marx: "Religion is the opiate of the masses" and Ted Turner: "Christianity is just a crutch for the weak, for losers."

Even as a "cultural Jew," my perspective/opinion of Christians was that they simply couldn't be trusted. At Hebrew school and among my Jewish friends and families, this was implicit in our understanding of the motivations of Christians: If the Gentiles were friendly and nice to us Jewish people, it was because they wanted to see Jews converted, that "they" did not accept "me/us" as a Jew, as a person of Jewish faith. The term "Jew" carried with it a negative connotation. So I grew up believing that at the heart of any kindness shown by Gentiles lurked their desire to proselytize us, to steal our *neshama yehudit*, our Jewish soul and identity. My "Jew-dar" was always up, always scrutinizing the actions and words of Christians.

It was Dorothy, the night receptionist, primarily, that I quoted Ted Turner and Karl Marx to. Nights at the dealership were quieter than the day shift, and she always had her Bible with her. I would often try to draw her into "discussions," which were not really discussions at all, rather just me spewing out a diatribe against her faith. I'd start by asking her why she believed in the Bible (though I really wasn't interested in hearing her answer). Then I'd continue with comments such as: "The Bible is just a bunch of fairy tales strung together by people who can't explain natural phenomena." I can't remember her response, but I recall her smile, her pleasant disposition and these five words she spoke to me during these months: "I am praying for you."

At the same time in another part of the city, Lisa had been praying for several years for her future yet unknown mate...praying for him to be a man of God, for his transformation and salvation if he was "out there," still unsaved. She was praying for me.

To numb the conscience-pricks from these known and unknown sources, I would turn on Christian programming after coming home from partying and bar-hopping, and laugh at the televangelists. I had no clue that the desperate void inside me could only be filled by Someone I had never met, but who knew me better than I knew myself. I would exhaust every other possibility and finally be broken before I would meet and begin to understand this Yeshua. There was something about Yeshua and His followers, however, that both stirred and agitated me. I didn't know it then, but God was provoking me to jealousy.

Transformed

As I sped through the last days of my prodigal/atheistic lifestyle, I occasionally had visits from my former live-in girlfriend, Melissa. She had recently given her life to Yeshua, and God had put me on her mind. The task must have been given by God Himself since there was no one else that I would tolerate talking to me about "religion." She seemed determined—actually thrilled—to share her experience with me.

When she told me that she had been "saved," I remember thinking, *Wow! She's been brainwashed! She's in some cult, and they're probably taking all her money, like one of those guys on late-night TV.*

But my heart was stone cold, my conscience was seared, and I couldn't understand anything she was trying to say. Although I didn't tell her at the time, I did see a definite change in her attitude—180 degrees, in fact. Even her countenance was radiant. She was full of joy and would light up every time she talked about Yeshua.

Up to this point, I had never read the Bible, but that didn't stop me from condemning it vehemently. To me, the Bible was no different from Greek mythology. The witness of Melissa's life, however, couldn't be argued. I later realized that what I was seeing was the Holy Scriptures written on her heart.

Day of Deliverance

I will never forget the date: April 21, 1987. Melissa stopped by my workplace, a Mazda dealership in North Miami, and invited me to lunch at a nearby sushi restaurant. She had not wanted to come, particularly since every time she brought up the subject of Yeshua. I would shut her down. This time, though, was different. It was a divine appointment; God had given her the exact words that my broken heart needed to hear. I was finally ready to receive Yeshua as my Savior and Lord. It wouldn't be easy, though.

As we sat there in the restaurant, I heard some things I had never heard before. Melissa explained that Yeshua had left a place of majesty in Heaven to be born in a dirty stable, that He came to earth, knowing that He would die a horrible death, then rose from the grave, conquering sin and death forever. The reason? Because He loved me that much. Because God the Father so valued me (us) that He paid the highest price to rescue me from a certain death sentence and an eternity in hell. That my name is engraved on the palms of God's hands. That He has always known everything about me—right down to the number of hairs on my head—and loved me anyway! That He had loved me even before the foundation of the world and now stood waiting with His arms wide open for me to come home.

Never had I known such love or that I could be the object of such affection. That this King would come as a servant and take the punishment I knew I deserved. I was amazed ... stunned.

As we sat there in the restaurant, I knew Melissa could see how deeply I had been impacted, and when she asked if I was ready to commit my life to Him, I declined, muttering, "Maybe some other time." Almost immediately, though, I literally felt like my insides were on fire!

Leaving the restaurant, we walked back to her car. She drove out of the exit of the parking lot. Perhaps unconsciously, she chose to take the back way through a residential neighborhood instead of the two-minute drive on the six-lane highway.

Within seconds, I heard a voice inside me: *If you don't do this right now, you may never get another chance. You may die in your sins and end up in hell!*

"WAIT A SECOND! PULL OVER!" I blurted out to Melissa, "WHAT DO I HAVE TO DO TO BECOME A BELIEVER IN YESHUA?"

She braked and brought the car to a sudden stop on the shoulder of the road. Even the route she had decided on, seemingly at the last minute, was divinely arranged. If she had taken the major highway, there would have been no opportunity to pull over. The moment might have been lost, and along with that, quite possibly, my salvation. Right there, on the side of the road, she led me in a prayer that would forever change my life.

It was the first time I had ever uttered a real prayer, other than the rote *Bruchas* in temple many years before. As I sat there with my eyes closed, I waited for what might happen next. What should I expect? Would there be lightning bolts, thunder, flashes of light, booming voices from heaven? I felt nothing different physically, but my friend promised to bring me an easy-to-read Bible before the day was out.

Hungry For The Word

Those next few hours at the car dealership dragged on interminably, and I wondered, with no small degree of paranoia, if my colleagues somehow knew of the life-changing decision I had made.

Later that afternoon, I was relieved to see Melissa's car pulling into the parking lot. She jumped out, hurried inside, and handed me my very first Bible—a blue paperback New International Version, which I still treasure today. I had no idea where to start. Before I could even ask, Melissa suggested that I begin reading the Book of John (*Yochanan*). She told me that the Holy Scriptures tell us that God gives wisdom to those who ask for it, so she advised me to first ask the Lord—to pray—for wisdom and the ability to understand what I was reading.

Amazingly, I really *did* believe, even before I had read a single page. I couldn't wait to get home and dive into this Book I had previously condemned. As soon as I arrived, I headed straight to my room, skipping dinner. Just me and my new Bible.

I sat down at my desk and turned on my reading lamp. When I cracked open the Bible, before even checking out the "Table of Contents," I was amazed to see that I had opened—supernaturally, I believe—to the Book of John: Chapter 1, verse 1!

I began to read. Slowly. Savoring the words . . . the Word:
In the beginning was the Word
and the Word was with God,
and the Word was God,
and He was with God from the beginning.

It was as if blinding light were streaming from the Bible, and I felt as if I were going to be blown backwards out of my chair by some unknown force, a wind of revelation. I was literally hanging onto the sides of the desk, the light still streaming upward from the open Bible. As I read on, I remember asking myself, *Why have I never seen this before? Why has no one ever told me?*

Melissa had inscribed Scriptures for me on the flyleaf of this Bible, among them this one:

> *Blessed are those who hunger and thirst for righteousness,*
> *for they will be filled.*
> ~ Matthew 5:6

As I devoured all 21 chapters of John that night, in my heart an insatiable hunger and thirst was kindled for more of His Word!

Sharing Yeshua

The next morning, when I entered the dealership, the stench of cigarette smoke immediately assaulted my nose. In those days, one could smoke in a public building; it had never bothered me before since I myself was a smoker. On this day, however—the first day of my new life—the pungent stench of cigarette smoke was nauseating. Then my ears were assailed by the coarse jokes and filthy language of my colleagues. Every one of my senses had been instantly transformed, and I found myself delivered from the desire to smoke cigarettes, snort cocaine, get drunk, use profanity, or engage in promiscuous behavior. Looking back, I'm amazed that God cleaned me up without my knowing or even asking. It just came. From then on, all I really wanted to do was feast on the Word. In six months, I'd read the entire Bible twice and was always seeking to share my newfound Good News with anyone and everyone who would listen. Not everyone was happy about the "new and improved" Hugh, though. My old partying friends took every opportunity to belittle, criticize, and make fun of me. Even my boss pulled me aside, advising me: "Anything in moderation is fine, but too much of anything is not good, even 'religion.'" After sharing my decision with my mom, she simply shrugged. "If it makes you happy and helps you be a better person ... but," she warned me, "don't tell your father about this as it will not go over well." I was in good Company. Yeshua said:

> *"If they hated me they will hate you also."*
> ~ John 5:18

Despite the resistance at my workplace, I had opportunities to share Yeshua. But even when my colleague, Doug, became a believer, I had second thoughts about remaining in the marketplace. I didn't want to hang out with a majority of unbelievers—I wanted to be surrounded by others who loved God as much as I did." During this time, many of my prayers were petitions for resolution of this matter—one way or the other. One day I met a fellow who was assistant pastor at a Hialeah church, so I asked him for advice. He told me something I had not considered before: that perhaps I was the only "light" the unbelievers I worked with might ever see. "You can stay in the salt shaker," he said, "or you can do what Yeshua commanded us to do—'go into all the world and make disciples of all men.'" It was the right word for the right time, and I received it gladly.

The Letter

One late night as I read and prayed, I thought about my father who was dealing with terminal cancer. I so wanted to share Yeshua with him. I knew my dad desperately needed Him, just as I had, and I felt the crushing weight of this burden for this one I loved.

Suddenly, I found myself with pen and stationery in hand, and I began to write:

"Dear Dad... (I watched as the pen moved across the page in a flowing script that was very unlike my usual "chicken scratch.") In this two-page letter, I wrote about what had happened to me, as well as the simplicity of the Good News and Yeshua's mission during His time on earth. I told my father that I had discovered it was not Yeshua or His true followers who were responsible for two thousand years of evil and violence against our people—that those people who called themselves "Christian" were anything *but*.

Most importantly, as the pen moved across the page, I read the beautiful script telling my dad how much God the Father loves him, paying the highest price—the very life of His only Son, Yeshua (whom the Christians call "Jesus")—to redeem him from the ravages of sin and eternal death. I mailed the letter the very next day.

My mother picked up the mail the day the letter arrived, but withheld it from Dad for a couple days. One night, when she couldn't sleep, she went into the kitchen where she had stashed the letter. Standing in the middle of the kitchen floor, she read it again.

Hearing that she was up, my dad awoke and called out to her, "What is Hugh saying?"

"I'm not talking to Hugh," she called back. "I know he's talking to you," Dad insisted." What's he telling you?"

With that, she went back to the bedroom and read the letter to him. While I didn't hear from my father regarding the outcome, I have a confidence from my heavenly Father that I will see my dad again in heaven—the New Jerusalem.

* * *

I also shared the Good News with my college friend and roommate, Mark, who had noticed the change in me. There was some early strife when our contrasting lifestyles clashed; I was saddened when he suddenly moved out of our apartment. What I didn't know was that the seeds planted had taken root.

Just a few weeks later, I received a call from him. He asked me if I was sitting down, because he had something very important to tell me—he had come to believe in Yeshua, had given his life to Him, and had made a complete about-face! We had great cause to celebrate. Instead of getting high on drugs, we were reaching new heights, thanks be to God.

Therefore, if anyone is (engrafted) in Christ (The Messiah),
he is a new creation (a new creature altogether);
the old (previous moral and spiritual condition) has passed away.
Behold, the fresh and new has come.
~ 2 Corinthians 5:17 (AMP)

I felt "fresh and new." So did Doug . . . and Mark. We were somehow totally changed. Almost overnight, God had not only done some serious housecleaning in me, He had recreated me. I was twice born!

· 5 ·

Matchmaker, Matchmaker

> ADONAI, God, said,
> "It is not good that the person should be alone.
> I will make for him a companion
> suitable for helping him."
> ~ Genesis 2:18 (CJB)

As I spent more time in prayer and meditation, I began to desire intimacy with the Lord, and I asked Him to fill me so that I would feel His Spirit within me. With that petition, I also laid down my compulsion to be romantically involved with a woman at all times. This old method of bolstering my ego needed to be replaced. I was learning to practice the presence of God. In His mercy and grace, I would soon find that He had a very special plan custom-tailored for me.

I had been a believer for only three months when two young women, Heather and Lisa, approached me after a service at my congregation. As they greeted me, I glanced at the darker-haired girl, Lisa. Her beauty so intimidated me, I had to look down, unable to mutter more than a sheepish "Hi." We exchanged "Nice to meet yous" before they walked away. Hardly my typical response when encountering attractive young women. God had transformed my demeanor and attitude into that of a gentleman, seemingly overnight. I didn't know it then, but Lisa had only recently broken off a serious relationship and was not looking to get involved in another one so quickly.

In recalling my first impression, I knew only that she had gorgeous, long, dark brown hair, with curls cascading past her shoulders, and the biggest, most expressive brown eyes I had ever seen. I later found out that Heather had already given Lisa the lowdown on me. If I had known that, I would not have been able to look into those innocent brown eyes at all.

Lisa: *My friend Heather told me that she had met the perfect guy for me. He was a new Jewish believer (strike one!), divorced (strike two!), with a young daughter (strike THREE! HE'S OUT!).*

"Not interested," I said.

"But you really need to meet this cute guy!" she insisted.

All I could think of was a recent visit from a pest control man two months earlier. He was not our regular exterminator, but I soon sensed that this was a divine appointment. He had a word from the Lord for me that day.

"You need to lay down your 'idol,'" he said. "You're obsessed with something, and you need to repent, surrender it, and let the Lord deal with it. Until you do, God cannot fulfill the desire of your heart."

He had no clue what my particular "idol" was, but I did, and when he asked if he could pray for me, I quickly agreed. As we prayed together, the Lord further revealed that my idol was the act of trying to find my future husband without relying on God. I wanted it, the way I wanted it, when I wanted it–which was NOW. But after this prayer, I repented and decided that I would do things God's way.

No sooner had I made this decision, though, than I jumped at the very next chance to accept a date with a man, my mind going into automatic over-drive: Is this the one, Lord? Is this the one? When there was no second date, I realized that I had broken my promise to God. Once again, I had tried to "help" Him, as if He were ever unaware of the desires of my heart—to marry a Jewish believer who would also be my best friend.

From that day forward, I decided that I would not get involved with any guy, no matter how cute he was.

Playing Hard to Get?

In the ensuing weeks and months, Lisa and I kept running into each other at meetings and Bible studies. One evening, upon arriving home from work, I was pleasantly surprised to see her car parked in my driveway! She had shown up for a Bible study held in the very home where I had been renting a room. I was convinced (incorrectly) that she had made a conscious effort to be there because of me.

Lisa: *I could not have been more shocked when Hugh turned up at the home group Bible study I attended. I had chosen it because of its proximity to my house. He seemed a bit taken aback, too.*

When he asked, "Hi, what are you doing here?" I replied, "I'm here for the Bible study. What are you doing here?"

He shrugged and said, "I live here."

I thought he was attractive, but instantly reminded myself of my promise to God--no dating, no begging Him, no dreaming if perhaps there was some chance that Hugh was the "one." In fact, I found that the Lord had instantly removed all those emotions—all the obsessing and fantasizing were gone.

Despite all my good intentions, everywhere I went, Hugh was there. I felt that perhaps he was "stalking" me. We both had the same circle of friends, so for months he was showing up at every event I attended. And he was the perfect gentleman—opening doors for me, pulling out my chair for me, and treating me with respect. But it was still very uncomfortable for me in view of my recent promise to God.

I felt Hugh liked me, but the feelings at the time were definitely not mutual. At the same time, I didn't believe in coincidence. The definition of "coincidence" is when God chooses to remain anonymous. I believe every event is God-ordained, a God-incident—no matter how seemingly small. So, the fact that Hugh kept showing up in venues where I happened to be? Hmmm. I'd have to mull that over . . . and pray some more.

Popping a Big Question

I finally got up the nerve to ask Lisa: "Hey, would you like to go to the movies or something?"

Her reply? "Hmmm, I don't think so…I'm moving my things into my brother's old room."

It sounded pretty lame to me, but it was actually the truth. Nonetheless, my imagination ran wild, and I was sure she was just looking for a reason to ditch me! Now I was confused… I was so sure that her interest in me meant more than just friendship, and I wondered whether I was out of God's will, considering my recent 100 percent commitment to Him alone.

I kept my feelings to myself and backed off a bit, but we kept bumping into each other. Slowly, we became really good friends, and I was able to answer her questions regarding the circumstances of my divorce. I assured her that I had not cheated on my ex-wife. Nor had I left the marriage because things were not "working out." Rather, the marriage was broken because of my ex's unfaithfulness.

Lisa: *Months later, we—Hugh, Heather, another friend, and I—were at a restaurant. Over lunch, Hugh and I were discussing our favorite wristwatch. It turned out we both liked the same type watch, right down to the blue lapis lazuli watch face!*

In that moment, God whispered to my spirit, Lisa, because you have been obedient and kept your vow, I am releasing in you a love and desire for this man.

Fireworks! That's when I fell in love with Hugh. In an instant! In the twinkling of an eye! Inexplicable, except through the Lord. As I looked across the table at Hugh, I felt such a deep love for him.

Midnight Confessions

Soon after that evening, we began talking on the phone regularly. A few weeks later, I confided in Frank, my roommate: "Frank, I'm in love with Lisa, and I have to tell her!"

He advised against that. Actually, what he said was, "You're crazy! Do you want to ruin a perfectly good friendship?"

I refused to be dissuaded though. So, one night, as Lisa and I talked on the phone, I ventured, "I need to tell you something."

"Okay...what is it? Are you okay?"

"Yes, sure, I'm really great...."

"Yes...?"

Another long pause on my end. "I like you," I finally croaked out, not knowing where I was going with this.

"Well, I like you, too."

"What I mean is . . . I *really* like you!" I exclaimed.

To which Lisa replied, "Well, I *really* like you, too."

Finally, after a brief awkward silence, I came out with it: " Okay, I don't just like you . . . I'm in love with you!"

I held my breath, waiting for her answer. After a few seconds that seemed like an eternity, I heard the words I had been hoping and praying for: "I love you, too!"

My heart and stomach did somersaults. She then told me that she had asked the Lord to give her a love for me if I was God's choice for her, and He had answered her prayer in the restaurant that night.

When I set eyes on her for the first time after that late-night confession, it was a bit weird; we were like teenagers in love. I remember talking for hours through the open window of her car as she sat behind the wheel. We talked for four hours. Then I leaned in and softly kissed her on the corner of her mouth for the first time—a moment that I have never forgotten, even nearly thirty years later.

Parental Approval

There were still obstacles to overcome. I had to clear her "guardians" and obtain the approval of both her mother and her spiritual dad, Alan. We planned a meeting two weeks hence—a meeting I would dread for every hour of that waiting time.

Lisa: *Early the next morning after our long post-confession date, I ran into my mom's room. Jumping onto her bed, I awakened her with the words,* "I'M IN LOVE WITH HUGH, AND HE'S THE ONE I'M GOING TO MARRY!"

My mom scoffed, "Every guy you've ever dated you think you're going to marry, so why should I think this one is any different?"

"Well, Mom, you and Alan just need to meet him," I said.

My mother was not especially pleased or enthused because of Hugh's past history. He was definitely not the kind of man she wanted her daughter to spend the rest of her life with.

It was time to fast and pray for God's perfect will. I told the Lord that I would not dishonor my mom or my spiritual head. I knew that I had to have their blessing in order for my marriage to start off on the right foot. I told no one that I was fasting, but every day I asked the Lord to change their hearts if I was supposed to marry Hugh.

Hugh: Two weeks later, in two different meetings, we all met. Fortunately for me, I was unaware of the gravity or potential impact of those meetings; otherwise, they may not have gone so well! To my immense relief, both "guardians" changed their minds, realizing that I was Lisa's match.

Lisa and I became inseparable, and on November 6, 1987, I proposed to her in the presence of her father.

"Mr. Schuster," I began, "I would like to have your permission and blessing to marry your daughter."

"Yes, please!" he exclaimed without missing a beat.

Ironically, the proposal took place at the same sushi restaurant where I had heard the gospel for the very first time on April 21 of that very year, and the location of our first date.

The Lord was giving me the desire of my heart.

* * *

Lisa and I married the following October in a storybook wedding at the Grand Bay Hotel, in beautiful Coconut Grove, Florida. As my best man, I chose Frank, my friend who had taken me in as a roommate. Frank had become a believer in Yeshua just one month before my own salvation experience. I had previously despised him and had considered him my archenemy. Why? He was the guy who had stolen my former girlfriend, Melissa—the very same girl who ended up leading both of us to Yeshua. As the Lord would have it, two adversaries were reconciled under the banner of love. I am still amazed at the irony . . . and the Lord's sense of humor!

Lisa is more than I could have ever dreamed of as a life mate. True, I had initially fallen in love with her beautiful brown eyes the very first time I had looked into them. Little did I know that shortly thereafter, I would fall in love with the wonderful woman peering out of those eyes—a loving woman of faith, integrity, conviction, values, and a deep desire for the things of God. She has always been a caring, supportive wife and a strong intercessor. We have been blessed with two beautiful daughters (that's three altogether!) and three grandchildren so far.

When we obey God and surrender to His will instead of ours, you can be sure that marriage—and all other relationships—will be what He intended them to be.

He is the ultimate Matchmaker.

-6-

The Chosen

But you are a chosen people, the King's cohanim,
a holy nation, a people for God to possess!
Why? In order for you to declare the praises
of the One who called you out of darkness into his
wonderful light.
~ 1 Peter 2:9

Jerusalem, if I forget thee...

As an atheist, I never thought much about Judaism or Israel. I identified with Jewish traditions, but that was about the extent of my connection. Raised as a non-observant Jew, I had been stuck in religious limbo. The fact that my mother was from a Catholic background made me feel somewhat like a "half-breed"; I sensed that I didn't really fit in anywhere.

Since I had never believed in God, I discarded religion. To be honest, I *despised* religion, which I considered to be contrived by cultures of superstitious people, even throwing into the mix the possibility of aliens, especially after reading *Chariots of the Gods* as a teenager.

While reading my Bible, I was surprised to discover that the Gospels had taken place in the land of Israel, that Yeshua lived His whole life there except for the time Joseph took Mary, whose name was really "Miriam," and baby Yeshua to Egypt to escape Herod's murderous plot to destroy all male children under two years of age. Learning that Yeshua and all of the disciples were Jewish impacted me tremendously.

Noting how the Old Masters had painted and sculpted the disciples in the great works of art, I had previously assumed that all the Gospel characters were Gentiles. In reality, the early followers were actually primarily Jewish believers, and the man whom much of the Church calls "St. Paul" was none other than the Gamaliel-trained Rabbi (Rav) Shaul. Yeshua's followers were not called "Christians"; the faithful were considered a sect of Judaism known as "The Way" (*HaDerech*). The holidays they celebrated were the Jewish holidays and the Feasts of the Lord (see Leviticus 23). The more I learned, the more I identified with my Jewish roots and, consequently, with the modern state of Israel.

A Hot and Dusty Land

In 1989, Lisa and I decided to make a trip to Israel. Not my first choice—even for a Jewish boy. I really wanted to go to Cancun and lie on a white sandy beach beside turquoise blue waters under the rays of a tropical sun. Lisa, however, had her heart set on a pilgrimage to the Holy Land.

As it turns out, Cancun took a beating from a major hurricane named Gilbert . . . so Israel it was. I still had no strong desire to go there. When I thought of Israel—although I knew it was the land of the Bible—I had visions of hot, dusty, desert country. Primitive. Even dangerous.

Another dynamic at work at that time was my father's deteriorating health. Two months before we were married, he had been diagnosed with inoperable lung cancer. He had undergone exploratory surgery, but the disease had already spread beyond remedy. The doctors were unsure how much time he had left, but they estimated about fourteen months or so. Having discussed my dad's situation with my mother, we were reassured that he was feeling reasonably well and, encouraged by my parents to go, off we went. On this trip, all my preconceived notions about Israel were about to be blown away.

From the moment we got off the plane, something inside of me clicked. We were met by the most amazing tour guide, Malcolm Cartier, whom God used to impart rich details about this ancient land . . . and something much deeper. As the tour bus lumbered along the road adjacent to the plains of Ayalon where Joshua pursued the Amalekites, as Malcolm shared with us, I had an instant connection with this tiny nation. Just as the Lord has built into each of our hearts a special place that only He can satisfy, I believe that Israel occupies a special place in every believer, especially those who are Jewish. And as I walked the path of the patriarchs, David, Solomon, the prophets, Yeshua, and His disciples, I began to feel that I belonged—that their blood ran in my veins and that this Land was my inheritance.

Psalm 137:5-6 reads:

> *Jerusalem, if I forget thee, may my right hand lose its skill,*
> *may my tongue cling to the roof of my mouth.*
> *If I do not remember you,*
> *if I do not consider Jerusalem my highest joy.*

I believe this is how God feels about His Land. Embedded in these words is the inexplicable desire to remain in this tiny, profoundly historical, blood-soaked spot that God has proclaimed as His eternal dwelling. And the more I explored this beloved Land, the more I felt His presence and felt my spirit drawn there.

As for the barren desert terrain? Every grain of sand is holy.

* * *

While in Cana, the town where Yeshua performed his first miracle—turning water to wine for a wedding when the hosts ran out of refreshments—we were tracked down by the U.S. Consulate. We were told that my father had taken a turn for the worse and had been placed in hospice care. We had a week left in Israel, and when I called my mother, she assured me that my father was expected to last another two or three weeks, and that he insisted we complete the trip. Something in my spirit changed; I felt like I was living on borrowed time, and thereafter, every moment of every day in this Land was that much richer.

I never saw my father alive again. When our flight landed in New York, Lisa checked in with her mother, who broke the sad news that my father had died at the exact time our plane had lifted off from Ben Gurion Airport.

Making Aliyah

On that journey, something was stirred in our souls, and the desire to make *aliyah* (the Hebrew word meaning "ascension," which is used when one immigrates to Israel) was now in the forefront of our daily thoughts. The more than seven hundred prophetic Scriptures about the Jewish people returning to their God-given homeland were illumined to us, and we read with new eyes:

> *"I will be found by you,"* says the Lord,
> *"and I will bring you back from your captivity;*
> *I will gather you from all the nations and from all the places*
> *where I have driven you,"* says the Lord,
> *"and I will bring you to the place*
> *from which I caused you to be carried away captive."*
> ~ Jeremiah 29:14

> *I will bring you out from the peoples and gather you*
> *out of the countries where you are scattered,*
> *with a mighty hand, with an outstretched arm,*
> *and with fury poured out.*
> ~ Ezekiel 20:34

> *It shall come to pass in that day*
> *that the Lord shall set His hand again the second time*
> *to recover the remnant of His people who are left.*
> *From Assyria and Egypt,*
> *From Pathros and Cush,*
> *From Elam and Shinar*
> *From Hamath and the islands of the sea.*
> *He will set up a banner for the nations.*
> *and will assemble the outcasts of Israel,*
> *and gather together the dispersed of Judah*
> *from the four corners of the earth.*
> ~ Isaiah 11:11-12

Along with Lisa's mother, Irene, we began to plan our *aliyah* in earnest. Thus began the challenges. At the time, we had no contacts, no friends or family in Israel. Furthermore, we had limited resources, and there were decisions that had to be made about when and where to settle. Also, we primarily spoke English and knew very little Hebrew (although I did remember some basics from Hebrew school). On top of all that, the Gulf War was raging, causing heightened tension in the Middle East. Even some of our friends cautioned us about making the move. But by March 1991, and against all odds, every obstacle had been overcome.

We had been introduced to a Messianic believer, Mark, who was a nurse in New York City. Mark split his time between Israel and New York, alternating a month in each place. He had already relocated his family to Ashkelon, which is just 13 km (8 miles) from Gaza. When we decided to make *aliyah*, Mark had invited us to stay in their home, and we took him up on his generous offer.

On April 15, 1991, we said goodbye to our friends and family in the U.S., and landed nineteen hours later at Ben Gurion Airport, Tel Aviv, where Mark was waiting to meet us. All along, we were praying about where we should actually settle, and after spending about a month in Ashkelon and Haifa, we felt led to move to Jerusalem.

There we found a lovely renovated apartment where we lived for about seven months in Rechavia, a suburb very close to Jerusalem's city center. Our upstairs neighbors were an elderly married couple, both doctors, who had a fascinating story. They had fled from Transylvania in Europe as part of the last clandestine *aliyah* before September 1, 1939, when Nazi Germany launched its attack against Poland, triggering World War II.

It took awhile to adjust to a totally different culture and language, and for the first six months, I attended an "Ulpan," a crash Hebrew course for helping new immigrants learn the language. As an American, I came to realize that the Israelis both embraced the West—and despised it. They loved the fashion and technology, but I quickly discovered that the last thing Israelis wanted to hear was, "We do it this way in America."

Walking Where Yeshua walked

Life in Israel was rich in experiences. We forged some wonderful friendships, many of which have endured. After the snows of the first winter, Lisa had an opportunity to go out into the desert and wonder at the explosion of flora. The desert floor blossomed beyond anything that had been seen in years, and it was as if God had treated them to a special viewing of His splendor.

> *The wilderness and the wasteland shall be glad for them,*
> *The desert shall rejoice and blossom as the rose.*
> ~ Isaiah 35:1

Living a frugal lifestyle while in Jerusalem, I loved walking around this city, bringing Psalm 48:12-14 to life for me:

> *Walk about Zion, and go all around her.*
> *Count her towers;*
> *Mark well her bulwarks;*
> *Consider her palaces;*
> *That you may tell it to the generation following.*

I especially enjoyed visiting the *shuk* (outdoor marketplace), with its pungent aromas of spices from the merchants hawking their wares, the savory fragrance of baking bread, the sweet smell of flowers and herbs. I relished our trips to the north to visit our good friends, Kent and Shawna Splawn, in Tiberius on the Sea of Galilee as well as the coastal areas surrounding Tel Aviv—Netanya, Herziliya, and down to Qumran, the Dead Sea, Masada, then all the way down to Eilat, bordered by Egypt, Saudi Arabia, and Jordan on the Red Sea. I was amazed that such a small nation could have such a big history.

For about a year, I worked at a gift shop and then as a volunteer coordinator with Bridges for Peace, a great pro-Israel international organization headquartered in Jerusalem, that supports and defends the nation of Israel, sharing both biblical truths and current events. Among the activities these volunteers were involved in were the day-to-day operations of a large food bank, establishing dialogue and relationships between Jews and Christians, both in Israel and the nations. BFP also ran a successful home renovation project in Jerusalem, Repairers in the Breach, which made minor repairs on the homes of elderly and poor Jerusalemites, free of charge. These projects were heartily endorsed by the municipality of Jerusalem.

During this time, I would frequently take a taxi into the Old City and visit the Garden Tomb, where Yeshua was buried for a short time. The Garden Tomb is located outside the city near the Damascus Gate. In those excursions, I met many Israeli Jewish taxi drivers, some of whom were third- and fourth-generation Jerusalemites who had never even heard of this garden. When they asked me what it was, I would tell them about the resurrection of Yeshua—that He had "borrowed" a tomb there for only three days!

In spite of all this, we found ourselves ill prepared to contend in the contests between the cosmic forces of good and evil. I sometimes describe this period of our lives as living under a high-voltage power line. We could feel the conflict in the atmosphere all around us and I, at least, did not understand the power of prayer. As we became aware of the battles that raged over Jerusalem in the heavenly realm, we would realize the absolute imperative of this kind of warfare prayer.

Battle Over Jerusalem

There are ancient territorial entities over this city, with demonic forces at work that are so strong you can feel their evil energy. I believe that the Holy Land is so important to God that He placed his archangel Michael there to protect this precious place, the homeland of the people He calls "the apple of His eye."

Psalm 122:6 reads: "Pray for the peace of Jerusalem…" but Jerusalem is soaked with the blood of countless thousands who have lost their lives as this city was attacked, conquered, and re-conquered many times throughout history. Why has Jerusalem been desired by so many? There are no significant natural resources, no strategic location or seaport there.

But in all the earth, this is the location Adonai chose as His dwelling place; it is the capital of the land He promised to His Chosen People. I believe that Israel is not the property of the international community, or any others. It belongs to God Himself. Unlike any other nation, He has marked out the geographical boundaries of this land, and He alone holds the title deed.

During our nearly four years there, we learned a great deal about real faith, as we were placed in situations where we had no other choice than to trust God to meet our daily needs.

The Test

It is interesting how people make plans for such important life events as conceiving a child as if we're the ones calling the shots. The real truth is that we can't do anything without God's help.

When we were attempting to start our family, Lisa had difficulty getting pregnant. Her doctor prescribed fertility drugs and she quickly conceived, but suffered from nausea, bleeding, and cramping—ominous signs in a pregnancy.

BarMitzvah September 1970, Miami Beach

Sibs: from left to right; Garen, Alvin Joel Jr, me, Jodi; Sept 1970

BarMitzvah reception with Dad and Mom

17 years old with new Kawasaki 900 motorcycle bought with my bar mitzvah money

1981, with daughter Lauren

The day I received Yeshua - Melissa's inscription in my first Bible

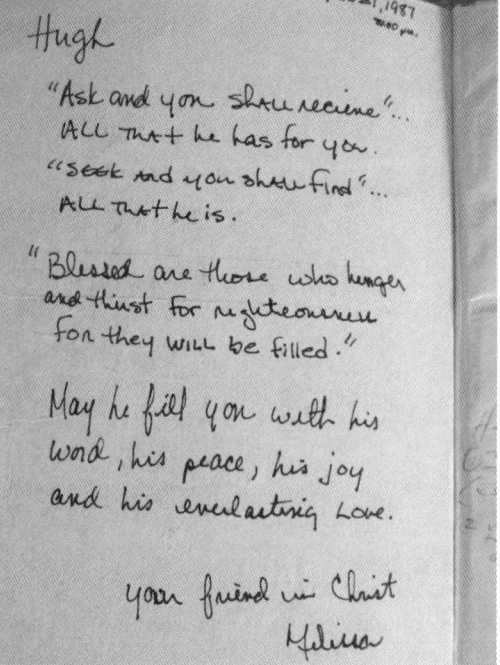

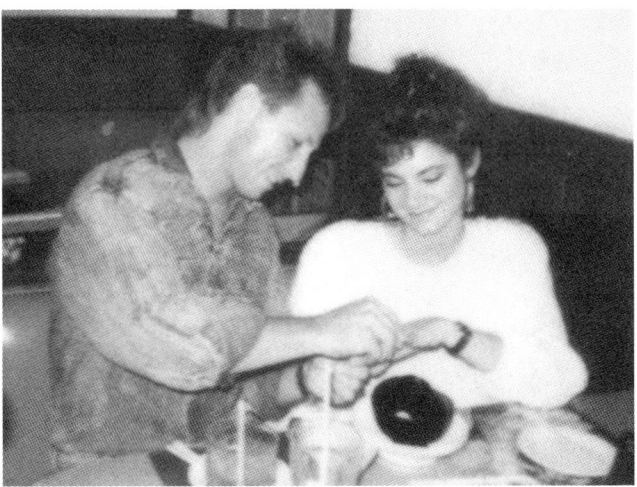
Engagement

With my parents and 7-year-old Lauren

Idol motorcycle summer, 2006

Lisa, my brown-eyed girl

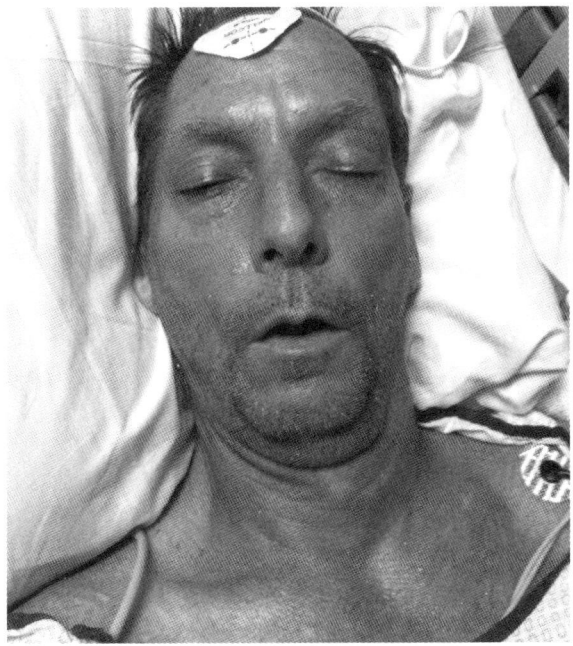
2012, Doctors are desperately trying to diagnose what's wrong...

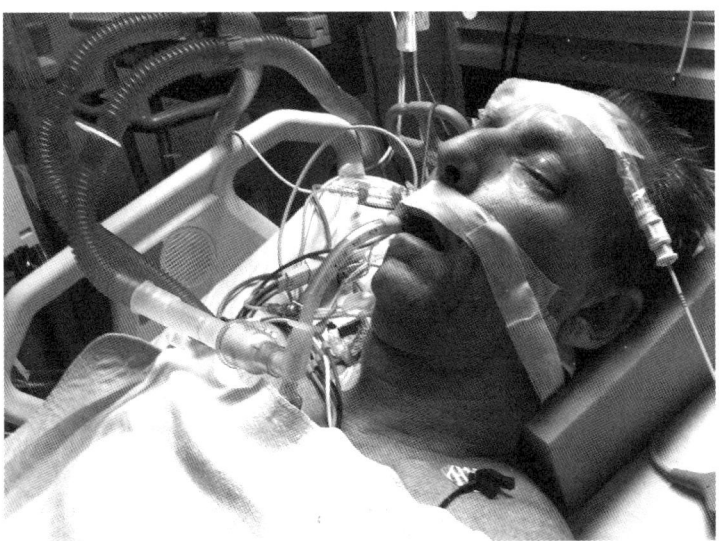
Post open-heart surgery- new mitral heart valve

When she was about six weeks pregnant, we decided to take a trip down to the Dead Sea to point out some historical sites to her brother Jeff, who had come to visit us in Israel. While we were there, Lisa doubled over with excruciating pain, and it was necessary to return to Jerusalem immediately. By the time we arrived, she was bleeding heavily, so we rushed her to the nearest—albeit the worst—hospital in the city. We were told that Lisa was having an "abortion." What the Israeli doctor meant to say was "miscarriage." Apparently, the two words have the same meaning in Hebrew, but it obviously had quite a different impact on us. We were heartbroken.

Lisa: *I knew from the get-go that these symptoms weren't good, but I have always had great faith, and so I believed that my situation would be turned around for good. But what happens when it doesn't turn around for our idea of "good"? Would I still trust the Lord? Would I still continue to believe His promises?*

In the hospital, Hugh was not allowed to be with me, and we had never been apart. While unknowingly in the process of a miscarriage, I was alone, frightened, unable to communicate (there were no English-speaking people there at that time). In the same room/ward with me were five other women—all Orthodox Jews—and I felt such a spirit of death in that place. I later found that abortions were routinely performed there, even though the hospital was located on the outskirts of possibly the most religiously observant Jewish neighborhood in the world (Mea Sharim).

All night long, I cried out to the Lord, and during that time, I lost the child I was carrying. This was the most traumatic event of my life to that point; I wept bitterly. I had always wanted a daughter, and to that end I had been collecting clothes for a baby girl. Still, I knew in my heart that this child I lost was a boy. I even named him "Zachary." Although this loss was crushing to Hugh and me, I still trusted God. He had a reason for taking Zachary straight to heaven, and I look forward to the day we finally meet.

In my despair, I said to the Lord, "If I don't have a baby by the time I turn thirty, I will be really depressed." Three months later, I was overjoyed to discover that I was pregnant again!

In spite of difficulties and nearly losing this child, on September 5, 1993, one week to the day before my thirtieth birthday, we welcomed our bat-tzion, Peri Yael Nemets. Peri means "fruit" in Hebrew; her middle name, Yael, is after the heroine in the book of Judges. She was born at Misgav Ladach Hospital, which was the only hospital we knew of that didn't allow abortions to be performed there. I could literally feel the difference between the two hospitals. While there was a deathly pall hanging over the first one, I noticed such a spirit of life and peace over Misgav Ladach.

Now our family was complete . . . except for Lauren, who was still with her mother back in the States.

-7-

Yeridah: Back To America

> *The people of Isra'el began grumbling against Moshe and Aharon;,*
> *the whole community told them,*
> *"We wish we had died in the land of Egypt!*
> *Or that we had died here in the desert."*
> ~ Numbers 14:2 (CJB)

A statistic compiled by the AACI (Association of Americans and Canadians in Israel) in the mid-1990s states that about 50 percent of Jews from North America who make *aliyah* end up moving back to America or Canada. The Hebrew word *yeridah* means to "descend or to go down." During our time in Israel, we moved four times in less than four years. The landlords would raise the rent, and since there was no rent control or limits, renters would be forced to move often as the rents escalated.

Although we made many friends, we never fully integrated into Israeli life. We weren't equipped for the intense battles we constantly faced. Think about it: Israel, in general, and Jerusalem, in particular, are the center of the world, and storms—of prejudice, persecution, and misunderstanding—are constantly swirling around them. More than one-third of all United Nations resolutions are against Israel. Our enemies deny our right to exist and have sworn to try to destroy us. I believe demonic forces drive such conflict.

For these, and other reasons, I always kept that "return-to-America" option open. One day when I was fed up and frustrated, I suggested this idea to Lisa and her mom, Irene, (who had also made aliyah with us in 1991). Together we made the joint decision to return. Let me say that we know that it was not God's will for us to "throw in the towel" that easily. We still believe God's promises and the prophecies bringing our people to the Promised Land, and I always felt that in His timing, we would again return to Israel.

God promised to be with us, but He never said life would be easy. So on December 31, 1994, we boarded a plane for America, nearly empty-handed. Our meager savings had been depleted; our belongings consisted of the clothing in our suitcases, some boxes, and a couple pieces of furniture. We rented an apartment right away. Thanks to a dear friend, Scott Brandon, I had a great job waiting for me as a car salesman at a wonderful family-owned Mazda dealership. I threw myself into my work, determined to make up for what I considered lost time.

Unfortunately, I began measuring myself against my contemporaries, many of whom had already established successful careers, owned homes, and had other material success. My faith took second place to my career as I struggled to overcome feelings of inferiority and poverty. On the plus side, we did become part of a congregation, which we attended regularly. God was not through with me yet.

Our Loss, Heaven's Gain

Soon after this, we were overjoyed to learn that we were expecting another child! But our joy was short-lived. Lisa had previously experienced difficult first trimesters, but this one was worse, far worse. She suffered through terrible morning sickness, so intense that one weekend, I rushed her to the hospital since none of the doctor's advice was working. Lisa was admitted, but I had to go to work that day as various tests were being run.

Around noon, I received a phone call from Lisa's OB/GYN, Dr. Klein, who left this message: "Something is wrong with the baby, but I can't tell you anything else. Meet me here at 5 o'clock today."

Lisa: *At the hospital, a technician wheeled me down for tests to determine what was happening. I remember the staff talking in hushed tones, but no one would tell me anything. Fear was rising in me; I was by myself, with my mind racing a million miles an hour. An endocrinologist came in for a consult, asking me some questions and talking with the sonogram technician, using medical terms I didn't understand. They kept pointing to the screen, all the while telling me nothing.*

After returning to my room, I cried out to God, but no answers or explanation would come until 5:30, when Hugh was finally there, along with my mom and dad. The doctor gave us the diagnosis: the baby had never developed normally, and I had a condition known as a "hydatidiform mole" or a molar pregnancy. This rare (1 out of 1000 pregnancies) disease occurs when the fertilized egg doesn't develop normally—the mass of cells never becomes an actual fetus and emits massive amounts of HGH (human growth hormone), which is why I had such morning sickness. The mole, if left undetected and untreated, could cause uterine cancer, and even metastasize.

The doctors immediately scheduled a D & C (dilation and curettage) to remove the growth; after surgery, I would have to have the HGH levels in my blood tested monthly, with strict warnings not to become pregnant anytime soon.

New Home! New Heart?

After living in that apartment for about a year and a half, we were miraculously able to purchase our first home, thanks to my wife's great pro-active faith. When she and her good friend Linda went house-hunting, those prayers paid off! We were starting over from scratch and did not have the finances for the down payment. Again, our friends, Scott and Linda Brandon, came to our rescue and loaned us what we needed. It was such a blessing to finally have a home of our own; so refreshing not to move every year! By this time we had been married for six years and had moved seven times. We were ready to put down roots and start raising our young family.

Although I had had some great experiences in Israel, I began to doubt whether we had actually made the right decision in going there in the first place. I felt that we would have been much further ahead if we had not moved to the other side of the world. But God had clearly opened the door and made the way for us. I have since come to understand that He was working His plan to build faith and character in us, and for the next ten years, I worked hard, investing my time, energy, and money as I developed my sales career.

This, too, paid off, and I was given great favor at my job, becoming one of the top Mazda salesmen in the country between the years 2000-2005. It seemed that everything I put my hand to was blessed. Eventually, the Lord also began to restore my relationship with my estranged oldest daughter, Lauren. I established my career, saved money, delighted in watching my 401k retirement account grow, and enjoyed a certain degree of affluence we had not known before in our married life.

* * *

Everything was improving . . . except my spiritual walk. A love of money and success started to replace the passion I once had for the Lord. The more I prospered, the further I departed from a meaningful relationship with God.

Rev. 3:16 reads:

> *So because you are lukewarm—neither hot or cold—*
> *I am about to spit you out of my mouth.*

Lukewarm . . . that was definitely me. This Scripture verse both terrified and convicted me. It was a dire warning and I knew it. I should have confessed and repented right then, but I kept my ever-increasing sins secret—or so I thought. There is no such thing as a "secret" sin where the Lord is concerned. We may be fooling some people, but God knows everything about us. He is right there, wherever we are, even as we are committing the most grievous sins.

If this is your situation, dear reader, if you are involved in things you think are "secret," I urge you to stop! Confess your sins and repent, because it's only a matter of time before they catch up to you!

As for my sins, the situation would only get worse. My heart was growing cold. I was feeding on a diet of worldly influences and was totally focused on myself instead of on Yeshua.

The tables were about to be turned.

Another New Beginning

After ten years of great prosperity in Ft. Lauderdale, Florida, Lisa and I began to contemplate moving to Tennessee. We were hurricane-weary, tired of living under the threat of incessant major storms. Some of our friends were considering relocating to the middle Tennessee/Nashville area for various reasons, and we were more than ready for a change.

We sold our Florida home and moved to Middle Tennessee, purchasing a beautiful six-acre property with a house we could live in until we built our dream home. There were some challenges. It took five months to sell our house, and prices had started to fall in our market. It sold in the nick of time, though, (God's mercy) just before the real estate bubble burst. God is so faithful—even if I wasn't!

While we were preparing for the move, I sent out my résumé to ten car dealerships in Nashville, received nine offers, and decided on accepting a position at the BMW dealership just as soon as we arrived in Tennessee.

* * *

The word *Tennessee* is thought to be of Cherokee origin, named after a Cherokee village "Tenasi," but there is no consensus as to the true origin or what the word actually means. Lisa and I would joke later as we struggled through various hardships that it means *"threshing floor,"* with lots of trials, tribulations, refining, and pruning dead ahead. We also later privately renamed our road, "Street of Broken Dreams," not just because of our struggles and losses, but because of other homes and properties on that road that had fallen into neglect and disrepair.

As for me, God saw things in my heart that had to be broken and re-formed. He could not use me the way I currently was . . . and so it began.

High-tech Idol

In the months preceding the move to Tennessee, I found myself in a state of discontent, yet believing I knew the perfect remedy for my happiness. I began to think about buying a BMW K1200LT touring motorcycle. It was the flagship of the line, gleaming and sleek, high-tech, beautiful, and huge. I wasn't just thinking about it, I had become obsessed with it. The idea of possessing this awesome machine consumed my every thought. Although I had owned six motorcycles during my high school and college years, this one was somehow different. I craved this more than anything, and I was determined to make it mine at any cost.

Never mind the not-so-small details that I had not ridden in 28 years, that motorcycle riding skills can become rusty. Unrealistically, I imagined Lisa and I touring interstate highways and byways together. I never stopped to consider the fact that I had two young daughters and a wife to consider.

I had placed the image of this machine as my laptop screensaver, as well as hanging a poster of it on a wall in my office. Although I did not want to admit it at the time, the bike had become an idol. I was completely convinced that somehow it would make me happy. I reasoned that I "deserved" it, and it was high time I treated myself. I thought about it all day, every day. When I told Lisa that I wanted to buy it ($23,500), she suggested perhaps I, at least should consider a less expensive one, but I wouldn't hear of it. When she saw that my mind was made up, she relented. So I struck while the iron was hot.

I contacted the dealer in Nashville, made a deal right over the phone, and gave the required deposit. The weeks between ordering the bike, moving to Tennessee, and getting to the dealership to complete the deal seemed to take forever. The day finally arrived. When I pulled up to the lot, it was there waiting for me, inviting and gleaming in the summer sunlight. I quickly finished the paperwork, declining the salesman's offer to go over the features and operating instructions. I did not yet have a motorcycle endorsement on my license and the dealership was fifty-two miles away from home, so next day, it was delivered to our house.

I could hardly wait to suit up for my first ride.

When the next morning finally came, I donned my riding gear, hopped on the motorcycle, and started the engine. Enraptured by the powerful sound, I revved up the motor and slowly proceeded down the driveway. I was so looking forward to this maiden voyage! When I stopped at the end of our long, unevenly paved asphalt drive, my right foot slipped ever so slightly in the gravel, the bike leaned just a little and, to my utter shock and disbelief, I realized that I was going to fall! This eight-hundred-thirty-five pound monster went over like the Titanic, with me on it, as my family watched in horror from the porch!

Three small but very expensive parts (it was a BMW, after all) on my brand-new motorcycle were broken in the mishap. The repair bill came to $600, and I hadn't even ridden one block! In trying to bring the motorcycle upright and not really knowing how, I had desperately grabbed a handlebar and some other part I wasn't meant to grasp, meanwhile yelling at Lisa to come help me. Lisa ran down and began pulling from the other side; somehow together we managed to bring it upright. My hopes for riding that day were dashed, and my confidence was severely shaken.

That gleaming black, expensive motorcycle sat in the driveway with a cover on it for about two weeks; I didn't ride it again until I completed a motorcycle safety refresher course, at Lisa's insistence. The cost of the course was another $250. To add injury to insult, when I attempted to lift the bike upright, I had damaged a vertebra in my back with the terrible pain persisting for some time. This injury would later come back to plague me.

In the eighteen months I owned the bike, it brought me absolutely no joy or satisfaction. I had this unshakeable sense of insecurity, never felt comfortable riding it. (I never had this sensation with any other motorcycle I had ever owned.)

Not surprisingly, I believe that because I had made this into an idol, God's anger had burned jealously against it. In His infinite wisdom, He turned something meant for leisure and enjoyment into a burden and stumbling block because of my deep obsession with it. The only One who can ever totally satisfy the desires of the heart is Yeshua. I knew that . . . but I didn't act like it.

New Kid on the Block

As I began my new job as a salesman at BMW of Nashville, I felt that I was not initially well received there by my new colleagues. I was used to being the "big dog" at my prior position in Fort Lauderdale, where I had been for almost thirteen years. Suddenly I found myself as the "new kid on the block" again. I had walked away from a large, loyal client base in south Florida and was starting over from scratch. I remarked to one colleague who was friendly to me that I had never experienced such a cold group of people, especially people who were supposed to be teammates; in reality, they viewed me as a threat and competitor. In the first six months I worked there, no other salesmen really ever spoke to me; some had even made side bets that I wouldn't last six months.

Before taking this position, I said that I had "prayed" about it, but the truth was that I had already decided that I would take the job without waiting on God for an answer. I had chosen this position over a different dealership, just because I wanted to—believing that selling cars there would be a piece of cake. I wrongly reasoned that there were no other dealers of that brand in town, and only five in the entire state of Tennessee. I surmised incorrectly there would be no competition. I never even checked to see how close the next dealer was to my showroom. As it turns out, there are many competitors, the nearest being only sixty miles away, just across the state line in Kentucky.

I had seen such great favor previously in my thirteen years with Mazda in Ft. Lauderdale, I presumed it would be a similar story at my new dealership. This, however, was not the case. And as time went on, we started to spend money that had been earmarked for savings toward our dream home.

I never considered my degraded spiritual condition nor the fact that I had created another idol—this one, my rollover IRA bank account from my job in Florida. I declared that I "trusted" God, but when I closed my eyes and looked way down deep inside myself, what I was actually putting faith, comfort, and security in was the money in that bank account. Of course I never mentioned any of this to Lisa. . . .

Business Proposition

After our first year in Tennessee, Lisa and I became interested in opening a restaurant franchise that was becoming popular at that time nationwide. We liked the idea of having our own business, and it seemed a great fit, especially with my previous restaurant management experience.

Soon after making the decision to explore the possibilities, we traveled to Florida to the company's home office, visited a couple of franchise-run units, and were excited about this entire concept. We considered this business opportunity carefully, prayed about it (casually), sought counsel from those we trusted, and asked friends to pray with us. No one gave us any negative feedback or any indication that this could be a risky investment. Although it would require a great commitment on our part, we believed that the Lord was directing us to this venture. In retrospect, I had really felt unsettled in my heart, but never brought it up to Lisa or anyone else until much later—too late.

We secured a $350,000 loan, obtaining the seed money by refinancing our home, which had been nearly paid off, and using the equity toward this venture. With the help of the franchise, we scouted several possible locations, finally settling on a great site in a new building in Franklin. Against the counsel of my father-in-law, who had extensive contract negotiating experience, we signed the lease with a personal guarantor clause in it. Over the course of six months, we undertook to fulfill the numerous items on the lender's closing checklist. This checklist required spending significant time, energy, and money (the $115,000 equity from refinancing our home), before the promised funds from the lender would be released. There were conversations and meetings with both the lender and property's agent, and others involved in planning the opening of the restaurant. We plodded forward.

With most of the vendors lined up and a construction company selected to complete the build-out, we had almost completed the endless closing checklist and were nearing the point at which the lender would disperse the loan proceeds to us when the economic situation began to look gloomy. A perfect storm was gathering on the economic horizon, and we were about to be caught in the middle of it.

Just weeks before finalizing, the lender's agent called me with news that turned my stomach: "Hugh, you have five days to close your loan."

My heart sank. Closing the loan in five days was impossible; it would take at least thirty days. The bottom fell out of this deal quickly after that. This especially devastated Lisa, and she sank into near total despair for a couple of weeks. The bulk of our equity money was up in smoke, and we were facing the possibility of being embroiled in a lawsuit with our would-be landlord, since we had signed a personal guarantee for three years rent on the lease.

As the weeks and months crept by, the real estate agent did not respond to us, and I became more curious and edgy as to why we had heard absolutely nothing from the landlords. Deep within my spirit, I sensed another storm brewing....

The Mitzvah

Nearly a year of stony silence from our landlords dragged by. The foreboding was potent. Then the other shoe dropped. One afternoon, the mailman delivered a certified letter notice. Immediately I felt fear rise up inside of me.

After a sleepless night, I drove to the post office and collected a thick, legal-sized envelope. I tore it open, my hands shaking, and pulled it out. In bold, black letters was the word **LAWSUIT**. My heart dropped, I felt nauseous, and I could barely catch my breath. We were being sued for $207,500 for not fulfilling the terms of our lease.

What followed was almost two years of continued legal wrangling between lawyers, without any real progress. The owners of the property refused to relent; they had a reputation for being astute, yet ruthless businessmen.

In 2011, Lisa and I began to feel a prompting in our spirits to do something that our attorney advised us was pure foolishness and dangerous to our case: we wanted to write the owners (plaintiffs) a personal letter. When we wrote this letter, we knew that the Lord's favor was on it. We called on the mercy of these businessmen, asking them to grant us a *mitzvah*, the Hebrew word meaning "good deed." Our attorney forwarded the letter to the landlords through their lawyer, and we waited.

Days and then weeks went by. Then, on the last day of Passover, which was also our youngest daughter's birthday that year, we received an email from our attorney. The email read: "Hugh and Lisa, see the opposing counsel's attached email. This is nothing short of divine supernatural intervention, seriously!"

Amazingly, the email stated that our letter had struck a chord of compassion, and if we would reimburse a relatively small amount in legal fees, they would withdraw any further action against us. A miracle delivered on the last day of Passover, the Jewish celebration of deliverance, against all odds! With no natural way out, God had made a way for us as surely as He had brought the children of Israel out of Egypt by parting the Red Sea.

But just as those rebellious children were not satisfied—even in the face of their miraculous deliverance—and had to wander through the wilderness for many years, so this stiff-necked son of Abraham had his own wilderness wandering dead ahead.

-8-

Mid-life Madness

If, then, the light in you is darkness, how great is that darkness!
No one can be slave to two masters;
for he will either hate the first and love the second,
or scorn the second and be loyal to the first.
You can't be a slave to both God and money.
~ Matthew 6:23-24 (CJB)

Approaching my 50th birthday, I was unhappy, disillusioned, and dissatisfied with everyone and everything around me. I can't begin to count the times I returned meals at some of the finest restaurants. Not hot enough. Not plated well. Improperly seasoned. A critical spirit had taken root in me. I had taken my eyes off Yeshua, and all contentment, peace, and joy eluded me. Opening doors that should have remained sealed shut, I soon found myself mired in the quicksand of a mid-life crisis.

I had stopped setting aside an intentional devotional time, no longer cultivating my prayer life or reading my Bible, and no longer listening to worship music. When I did crack open my Bible, it was out of a sense of duty. I hurried through the reading, seeing only words on a page. It was years later that God gave me the visual of a stony heart off which God's Word ricocheted in those days. The remedy for a heart of stone is found in Jeremiah

31:33: "I will put my laws in their minds, and I will write them on their hearts. I will be their God, and they will be my people."

I had a seemingly happy countenance everywhere except at home. My façade may have fooled everyone else, but Lisa and my children caught the brunt of my pain. I was miserable, by my own doing, and I was dishing out this misery to the ones I was supposed to love the most. I spoke cruel, hurtful things to these dear ones. Slowly, but surely, I'd drifted far, far from home.

Lisa: *It was probably a few years before we moved to Tennessee that I started to notice subtle changes in my husband. Instead of an occasional alcoholic drink when we went out, he'd have several. Very unlike the man I married, one who basically never drank liquor at all.*

More troubling was his language—crude, coarse jokes laced with sexual innuendo. And the music he listened to had shifted from worship and praise to secular. He no longer wanted to be involved in activities having to do with the Lord, and told me he wasn't interested in being a part of our congregation anymore, even though he was serving as head usher.

I realized that our marriage was headed for rough waters. When a person loses his first love—the Lord—you can look for trouble with a capital "T." That's exactly what happened to us.

The move to Tennessee only made things worse. Hugh didn't like his new job—and no wonder! He'd left a great position—and his entire client base—back in Florida, where he'd been the top man for years. Here he was starting all over . . . at the bottom. More disappointing, he was working long hours and making hardly any money.

By the time he got home from work each night, all he did was complain, yelling at the girls and me. Either the laundry wasn't done to his satisfaction, or he didn't like the meal I'd prepared for dinner, or something the kids were doing annoyed him.

To combat the problem, I decided that the girls and I would turn off the TV before he walked in the door, have everything in its proper place, and try to stay out of his way so that there would be nothing to set him off. However, the Hugh I was now living with had morphed into someone I no longer knew or liked. I sensed the darkness that had overtaken him.

I felt as if I were sleeping with a stranger.

As time went by and things continued to worsen, I realized that all I could do was get on my hands and knees and cry out to God, morning and night, day after day. Our cord of three strands—Hugh, the Lord, and I—was severely frayed, and the only One I could cling to was God Himself. Inside, I was carrying this terrible secret, one that I dared not share with another human.

We'd always had the "perfect marriage," or so everyone thought. We were two peas in a pod, but now Hugh had gone haywire. I told him we needed to get counseling, and to my surprise, he agreed. I began to fast and pray for God to intervene before the counseling session with our pastors. But even the session brought no results.

My prayer now was that God would either change him—or take him.

One thing I've learned in my walk with the Lord is that when I simply don't know what to do or where to turn, it's time to get on my hands and knees and cry out to Him. In almost every situation where I have fasted and prayed, the Lord has answered me remarkably quickly.

*　*　*

One night while Hugh was taking a shower, the detective in me kicked in. I grabbed his cell phone to see what I could find out. I was convinced that he was having an affair. When I tried to access the phone, I was blocked by a password, which immediately sent up a huge red flag. (Another tip: If your mate has password-protected their phone and not told you the code, there may be cause for concern. After all, if we are "one flesh," there shouldn't be any secrets.)

I felt sickened and waited for Hugh to step out of the shower. The moment he reached for a towel, I confronted him flat out: "Are you having an affair?!"

"Wh-what are you talking about?" he stammered.

"Your phone is locked! What's going on?"

"Why are you checking up on me?" he yelled.

"I'm your wife! I have every right!"

He was evading me, refusing to look at me, while I followed him around the bedroom, demanding an answer. He walked back into the bathroom, and as he turned and finally made eye contact, he uttered the most dreaded, earth-shattering words a spouse could ever hear: "I DON'T LOVE YOU ANYMORE! I FEEL ABSOLUTELY NOTHING FOR YOU!"

I felt like someone had just jabbed a knife in my heart. My marriage of more than 21 years flashed before me. Was it over? Were we headed to divorce court? When I broke down and sobbed, Peri, our middle daughter, came running in. "What's going on here? Are you guys getting divorced?"

"Your mother and I just had a little disagreement, that's all," Hugh quickly answered. "Everything is fine."

When Peri began to cry, he apologized to me. "Sorry, Lisa, I didn't mean what I said…"

But the damage was already done.

After Peri reluctantly shuffled off to bed, Hugh confessed his porn habit. . . .

Many believe that adultery only takes place when a spouse engages in a physical act with another person, but the truth is that pornography is nothing short of adultery. How do I know? Yeshua said that "whoever looks at a woman lustfully has already committed adultery with her in his heart" (Matt.5:28).

* * *

A short time later, we made a trip to Florida for a family reunion. At a party one evening, I suggested we leave early with the kids, fearing that Hugh would use this opportunity to drink heavily.

He refused. "If you want to leave, then leave, but I'm staying!"

I drove to the house where we were staying overnight with relatives, and after putting the girls to bed, I started to pray, "Lord, please let Hugh get so drunk that he gets sick and never wants to touch another drop!" God answered that prayer quickly because only a few hours later, it took two guys to carry him into the house!

I was up, still praying when Hugh stumbled into the bedroom. No sooner did he lie down than he got back up, retching. He vomited all night long, and at one point, he was curled up on the shower floor with the water beating down on him. He was so sick he didn't get out of bed till around two the next afternoon.

Somehow God gave me the grace to remain quiet through this episode, and to show my husband only love and compassion. Hugh told me that afternoon that he was done drinking hard liquor.

In all the years I had known him, I had never seen him stone-drunk like this before, and I believe it was because of those prayers that I have never seen him like that again.

We headed back to Tennessee a couple of days later with much uncertainty. The Lord had instructed me to be quiet, without nagging or arguing. Years later, my husband confided in me, "Your silence at that time was a better tool for the Lord to work in my life than anything you could've said to me." I'm grateful God gave me the grace to be obedient to His instruction.

But the struggle was far from over. I continued to cry out to the Lord. Tears were my constant companions. I felt broken, ugly, and vulnerable. I never felt so alone in all my life, with no clue as to what the final outcome would be. But I knew that I could not divorce Hugh and that I had to fight for our marriage.

Again, it was the Lord answering my prayers that gave me the strength to hang on.

… -9-

The Awakening

But everything exposed to the light is revealed clearly for what it is, since anything revealed is a light.

This is why it says,"Get up, sleeper! Arise from the dead, and the Messiah will shine on you!"

~ Ephesians 5:13-14 (CJB)

Summer, 2010

Things continued to spiral downward. After nearly ending my life in my parked car that May evening, I stumbled through the next two months in a fog. Some have called it "the dark night of the soul." Emotional fatigue and emptiness were all-consuming. I could find no relief; peace and joy eluded me.

Deep inside myself, I desperately wanted restoration. To feel the breeze of revival over my life. To recover the joy of my salvation. I had tasted of the Lord, and He is good. Very good. I had to find Him again. Had to know that He hadn't abandoned me.

"If We Ever Needed You"

In mid-July, after a frustrating day at work, I got into my car for the thirty-two-mile drive to my home in the country. On this particular day, I did something that had become uncharacteristic for me at that time in my life; instead of turning on my usual rock or country music, I cued up a Christian song by the band Casting Crowns. The song? "If We Ever Needed You." On impulse, I had downloaded this song from iTunes just that morning.

I have come to realize that when the God of the Universe is pursuing a person who has lost their way, He will go to any length, using anything and everything—His Word, another person(s), a t-shirt, bumper sticker, billboard, a fortune cookie, and in my case, a song prepared exactly for this moment—to reach the lost one. When I hit the PLAY button and the words of the song came forth, the Spirit of God (*Ruach Hakodesh*) fell heavily on me, shattering my brittle, hardened heart. As I began the drive, I cried out loudly, begging God for forgiveness. Hot tears flooded my face, and sobs of repentance wracked my body. My car limped along in the right-hand lane, my usual forty-minute commute morphing into an hour and a half.

The song played over and over, and I struggled to keep the car in the lane, one hand on the steering wheel; the other, clutching a handful of tissue. The tears continued to flow freely while I mopped my eyes and running nose.

Gently, my heavenly Father began to pour a balm of healing and cleansing over me and, for the second time in my life, I was set free from pornography addiction, alcohol abuse, and suicidal thoughts. He showed me the error in what I had done—my sins—revealing to me that I had erected many idols. I had piled them so high that I could no longer see God. Furthermore, I had tuned in to the cacophony of worldly noise, which had become so loud I could not hear His voice anymore. In the midst of this recital of my failures, my Father whispered that He had never stopped loving me, nor had He turned His back on me. No, it was I who had stopped listening and turned away from the One who loved me so furiously. Taking my eyes off Yeshua, I had veered off course, and into dire straits. So great was the revelation that it took me weeks to begin to unpack it or to share fully with anyone else—even Lisa.

When I arrived home, I managed to get out of my car and staggered up to the front door. Lisa met me, looking worried....

Lisa: *When I opened the door, Hugh was standing there. His eyes were swollen and bloodshot, and he was holding a soggy wad of tissue the size of a softball. He was sobbing.*

"Where have you been?" I probed. "What happened to you? Did you get fired?"

"No..."

"So... what's going on?"

After he finally caught his breath, he slowly croaked out an explanation, one word at a time. "I... God... showed... me..."

"God showed you what?"

It took him about twenty minutes or so to get out a complete sentence. Apparently, Hugh had had an encounter with God on the way home as He poured revelation into him.

That night the Lord gave me back my husband.

My prayers were answered!

God is faithful.

* * *

I mumbled something about God breaking through to me. Still sobbing, I held on to Lisa as I pleaded for forgiveness. It was the beginning of our restoration.

Lisa's prayers for my repentance and return—my *tshuvah* (pronounced choo-VAH)—with God's help, had been answered. The message of how much He abhors idolatry, how much He loves us, and how jealous He is for relationship with us, is a major theme in His Word. God's desire is that we run hard after Him—seek, love, and know Him with every fiber of our being.

I had been "ruined." As Paul said, "I counted it all as rubbish compared to the riches of knowing Him" (Philippians 3:7-8). I was aroused from slumber and could actually hear God's voice. In a way I felt like Lazarus, Yeshua's friend, who died and after three days in a tomb, came forth when Yeshua called his name. Like Lazarus, I had been bound by the grave clothes of my sin and sorrow. Now they were ripped away and I was walking in new life.

Restoration

The evening of July 19, 2010, was like a glorious daybreak after a long, dark winter's night for my wife, my children, and for me. The oppressive misery, tension, and darkness that had shrouded our home was replaced with peace, joy, and healing as the *Ruach HaKodesh* took up residence in me again.

Every aspect of our marriage blossomed. Lisa and I fell in love with each other all over again. Slowly her trust in me was rebuilt, and my daughters' emotional wounds—especially teenaged Peri who bore the brunt of those dark years caused by my cruelty—healed. They enjoyed being with me, and I treasured my time with them. As I learned to follow the Lord's direction and leading, I was better able to lead my family.

Lisa had been planning to take Elli and Peri and some other friends' families to International House of Prayer-Kansas City (IHOP-KC) the next week to attend a teen summer camp. My wife was also looking forward to spending time in the Prayer

Room, a 900-seat auditorium where continuous 24/7 worship and prayer had been underway since 1999. When she'd first mentioned this to me the month before, I'd had no interest in going there. I'd used the excuse that I had no vacation time left. "Everyone knows that salesmen don't just take off at the end of the month."

But after July 19, everything changed. I knew I needed "face time" with the Lord. That week in Kansas City was a time of real refreshment, and I basked in God's presence. There would be a number of other trips there in the next two years. The worship that flowed from anointed IHOP worship leaders such as Misty Edwards, Jon Thurlow, Laura Hackett (Park) and so many others was an important part of my further growth and healing.

One of the best aspects of the 24/7 Prayer Room is the ability to webstream live audio/video on the computer or any mobile device. And soon after returning to work, the 24/7 stream could be heard from a number of offices in my showroom as I shared this resource with others I discovered were believers. I was no longer a "secret agent," no longer ashamed of the gospel or my Messiah. I felt the compulsion to share the same love with others around me that my Father had lavished on me.

I began to pray for divine appointments and started reaching out to those I worked with—and not just my colleagues. I made it a point to stop in and chat with technicians, the car detailers, the ladies upstairs, my managers—expressing genuine interest in them and their lives. Many opened up to me, but others remained distant and detached, much like I had been.

Another thing that bothered me was the 55-65 hours a week my job as a car salesman demanded, keeping me away from home. I began to pray, without preconditions, that God would give me more time with my wife and children. I had no idea how He planned to answer that prayer, but I would find out soon enough.

The Seal

Here's something I have learned the hard way: Never say never. When you do, the Lord will bring the challenge of those vows right to your doorstep. I had often declared that I would never get a tattoo. I considered them to be trashy and a waste of money; besides, they are permanent.

One day, however, I was listening to the Misty Edwards song, "You Won't Relent," and the lyric: "I'll set you as a seal upon my heart, as a seal upon my arm, for there is love that is as strong as death, jealousy demanding as the grave...." It was then the Lord spoke to me: *You are to get a tattoo, a seal, marking yourself with the Hebrew inscription: "Kadosh L'Adonai," which means HOLY TO THE LORD.*

He told me that this inscription was what marked vessels dedicated to holy service in the First and Second Temples. He also told me:

> *Although you were a battered, dirty, and burnt-out vessel, you are being restored and rededicated.*
> ~ Zechariah 14:20-21 (author's paraphrase)

While I was at the tattoo parlor, the Lord further instructed me that this seal was to be large and prominent, taking up almost the length of my right inner forearm, from wrist to elbow. *Many people will be drawn to you and inquire about it,* He said. *Many doors will be opened for you to share your testimony.* True to His word, that is exactly what has happened.

But there was a secondary reason why this tattoo was to be placed specifically on my inner forearm. This is the area of the body where Jewish inmates were marked for death at Auschwitz, Dachau, and thousands of other Nazi death camps during World War II. My new tattoo spoke of holiness and life, restoration and redemption.

I must say, the procedure was quite painful, as I understand now that the inner part of the forearm is extremely sensitive. Even in that there was a purpose; the pain served to help me understand on a very small scale what Yeshua must have endured for me.

Hidden Treasure

After my awakening, the Lord brought to my memory something I had not thought of in thirty-nine years. Not once. I remembered an event that occurred when I was a teen; as I recalled the incident, a spiritual light bulb came on.

When I was about fourteen, growing up on Miami Beach, I went to the beach on Collins Avenue and 22nd Street with my brother and some friends near a small hotel, The Hotel Chanin, owned by my friend Drew's family.

While we were snorkeling, we discovered sand dollars (a type of starfish) blanketing the ocean floor in shallow waters. They had no monetary value, but they were cool to look at, and we enjoyed collecting them. So we paddled out about fifty yards off the beach in approximately ten feet of water with two small, four-foot-long canvas rafts.

The outline of their shapes was visible just beneath the sand as we dove down in the crystal-clear waters. It was easy to snatch up the sand dollars, but unknown to us, the tide was going out, and the rafts were not anchored. Without an anchor, we were subject to move with the tides.

Every time we came back up with our treasure, the rafts had drifted ever farther away from shore—and from us. When we finally turned around and looked toward the shore, we realized we were close to half a mile from the beach. By now, we could barely make out the shoreline, and the people looked like ants.

The swim back was long and arduous as we struggled against the powerful tide. Thankfully, we had brought fins, which enabled us to make the return trip more easily. We had drifted almost too far away, and our booty—the sand dollars—had to be returned to the sea so that we could use the rafts as lifeboats. In spite of our foolishness, we had been divinely protected from drowning . . . and sharks! Hammerheads, makos, and tiger sharks are common in these waters; because the ocean was so calm that day, our splashing would have been easily detected by any shark lurking around.

The Lord showed me how easy it is to become so engrossed in chasing after worthless things, we take our eyes off God, who is the only immovable One, the One who cannot be shaken. Without keeping Him as our focus, we are apt to stray far from the safety and security we often take for granted. And we may substitute cheap imitations for the true treasure, hidden in Him.

Supernatural Lasik

From the time I was about fourteen, I needed to wear glasses, mostly for reading. As time went on, my eyesight continued to require the aid of corrective lenses, and in my mid-thirties, I began to wear contact lenses full time.

One morning a few weeks after my *awakening* experience, just after we returned from our first trip to the International House of Prayer, Kansas City, I was getting ready for work. As I put my contact lenses in, I realized my vision was blurry. I took the contacts out, inspected them, cleaned them, and put them back in, only to discover that I still couldn't see clearly. Thinking that perhaps it was time to see the ophthalmologist and get a new prescription, I removed them and laid them aside.

As I peered about the bathroom, I realized excitedly that something curious had happened. For the first time in twenty-five years, I was seeing perfectly without glasses or contacts! To be sure of it, I grabbed my Bible and looked at the fine print. my hopes were confirmed: My eyesight had been restored! I ran to tell Lisa about this miracle, and as we thanked God together, I heard the voice of the Lord telling me: *"The supernatural restoration of your natural vision is a sign to you of the supernatural spiritual vision I am giving you as you walk with Me."*

It was just two months later that He commissioned me to start blogging—"Be Encouraged"—at www.kadoshladonai.blogspot.com.

The Accidental Writer

When the Lord spoke to me: Hugh, *I want you to start writing a daily devotional blog,* my knee-jerk reaction was, "Lord, but I'm not a writer!" Nor had I ever aspired to be a writer.

His response: *I didn't ask you if you were a writer! Just write what I tell you to write—nothing more, nothing less.*

So on October 13, 2010, this "accidental writer" penned his first blog post. I began to share what God would give me for the blog that day with colleagues and clients alike. I don't know why, but I was surprised when someone would tell me or email me that what I shared that day was exactly what they needed to hear.

In late December, 2010, when Lisa and I were at IHOP-KC (International House of Prayer, Kansas City), a winded young man ran up to us and said, "I saw you all earlier and the Lord gave me a word to deliver to you, and I didn't...but now, since I've seen you again, I ran to catch you. Here's what the Lord told me to say: 'I (the Lord) am giving you a fresh new word for the body of believers. It is unusual, different, and much-needed." Turning to Lisa, he said, "Oh, and He wants you to know that you have beautiful feet." As we stood there, our mouths gaping open in amazement, he said, "Well, that's it! See you later." We never saw him again and to this day, we wonder if he was actually an angel.

I am still blogging at www.hughnemets.com and my original blog at www.kadoshladonai.blogspot.com. It has been a lesson in perseverance. God is teaching me that when we are obedient, it doesn't matter how "incapable" we might perceive ourselves to be.

What really matters is how the Lord sees us, His divine creations. We are uniquely designed by Him for His purposes.

> *You have seen my potential from before I was born.*
> *Every day of my life was recorded in Your book.*
> *Every moment was laid out before a single day had passed.*
> *How precious are Your thoughts about me, O God.*
> *They cannot be numbered!*
> ~ Psalm 139:16-17 (author's paraphrase)

The many messages my Father has given me to write and share with others are often the exact things I myself need to hear. I have learned not to make presumptions about the tasks He gives me. I have no idea how the words I write will touch the hearts of those who read them. My responsibility is to be faithful to share the messages, the thoughts God often drops into my spirit.

> *The Word goes forth and never returns void,*
> *but will accomplish what He desires, achieving His purposes.*
> ~ Isaiah 55:11 (author's paraphrase)

I have been amazed to discover that my writing has made its way to people all over the world. Readers forward these posts on to others, and they forward them on again. I have learned my part is simply to be obedient and not worry about the details. God does the rest.

Something's Going On . . .

I continued to write, continued to grow in understanding God's great and furious love. Things were also going well for me at work finally, but in the spring of 2012, I began to feel a strange fatigue. For two years I had been in the best shape of my life-- but suddenly my condition began to change. A short walk five hundred yards up a three-degree grade to the employee parking lot would leave my legs feeling as if they were made of cement, and I could barely catch my breath.

Back in May, I had undergone a routine colonoscopy. As the anesthesiologist examined me before the procedure, he had registered concern when checking my heart with his stethoscope. When he finished, he stepped back and said, "Did you know you have a significant heart murmur? You should see a cardiologist immediately."

I shrugged it aside and later told Lisa, "That man doesn't know what he's talking about. There is absolutely no history of heart problems in my family."

He did know, though. He knew exactly what he was talking about. My condition worsened through that summer of 2012. Little did I know that a deadly infection was developing on the interior lining of my heart, and a resistant, insidious bacteria was already at work damaging the muscle, causing it to become abnormally enlarged.

I had given my heart to Yeshua. Now I would need Him to heal it and give it back to me.

-10-

Stricken

> *In fact, it was our diseases he bore,*
> *our pains from which he suffered;*
> *yet we regarded him as punished,*
> *stricken and afflicted by God.*
>
> *But he was wounded because of our crimes,*
> *crushed because of our sins;*
> *the disciplining that makes us whole fell on him,*
> *and by his bruises we are healed.*
>
> ~ Isaiah 53:4-5 (CJB)

Apparently, the enemy wasn't through stalking me. On July 29, Lisa rushed me to a local ER with a fever of over 103 degrees. My entire body was screaming in pain. I told Lisa that on the 1-10 pain scale, I was an "11!" Incredibly, the attending ER doctor found nothing wrong, speculating that it might be the flu, and sent me home to "sleep it off" after giving me an injection of Toradol and a shrug of his shoulders.

Less than thirty-six hours later, in the pre-dawn hours of July 31, Lisa phoned our neighbors and close friends, Jesus (pronounced HAY-soos) and Georgia Hernandez. I was acting aggressively; I was agitated and irrational. For hours I had been exhibiting odd behavior. I would lie down for a few minutes and then head toward the bathroom, where I shuffled about restlessly, dousing my face with cool water from the sink. While I was in there, I tinkered with the toothbrush stand, the faucet handles, and was about to remove the toilet tank lid when Lisa pried my hands off.

From there, I wandered toward the living room, and thinking I was in the bathroom, almost urinated on the coffee table. Lisa intervened just in time! Repeatedly, she tried to engage me, to question me as she struggled to figure out what was actually happening. At this point, I was incoherent, babbling unintelligible words. In the 25 years Lisa had known me, she had never seen me with any illness worse than a bad case of the flu. She thought that perhaps the effects of the Toradol shot might be interacting with the other meds to account for my outlandish behavior. But in her heart she knew better—it was much worse than that.

Elli, our then eight-year-old daughter, was now awake and, hearing the commotion, rushed out of her room to find out what was going on. Reassuring Elli that everything was just fine, Lisa sent her back to bed. But my wife was convinced that everything was not "just fine." In my pain and frustration, I had pushed her. Never in all those years had I shown physical aggression toward my wife and three daughters, and she was frightened. She locked me in the bedroom for my own safety—and hers.

In the midst of all this, Lisa spent at least twenty precious minutes on the phone investigating which hospital would actually take our insurance. With four possible choices—all of them forty minutes to the north—she prayed, "Lord, please direct me to the right hospital!" Within minutes she had her answer as she heard the voice of the Lord whispering in her spirit: *Centennial Hospital*.

With that decision made, she then tried to get both of us dressed. No luck. I was just too agitated and uncooperative.

Thankfully, our friend Jesus arrived a few minutes later. (I've often thought how like Yeshua to send His counterpart to comfort me—my Cuban friend with the same name!) Jesus took both my hands in his, looked me in the eye, kissed me on my forehead, and calmly reassured me that everything was going to be all right. He told me that he loved me, and I immediately calmed down.

Miraculously, the two of them were able to get me out of the house and into the van. Lisa somehow managed to keep her composure while racing those forty miles to Centennial Hospital in Nashville. Jesus stationed himself next to me, vigilantly guarding me to prevent my attempts to unbuckle my seat belt and jump out of the speeding van.

Meanwhile, Georgia Hernandez took Elli over to their house, where she was watched over by Georgia and Jesus' daughter as we headed for the city. Upon our arrival at Centennial's ER, Dr. Karen Younghale immediately attended me. There I would eventually spend the next 28 days, fighting for my very life.

Glimpse of Glory

Between hospitalizations, as I languished on my sickbed at home after returning from the local ER, something happened that would change everything. Lisa had put on some of my favorite worship music. The song, "Storm All Around You," by Jon Thurlow, softly began to play. As I lay there listening, I heard the voice of the Lord beckoning me, *Come up here*. And He took me up into the Throne Room of Heaven.

Lisa and our daughter Elli were at my bedside, and I began to describe what I was seeing in that exalted moment. Constantly circling around the throne of the Most Holy God were seraphim, heavenly beings with huge, gleaming white wings. With tremendous power in the movement of their wings, they made a great swooshing sound. Awesome to behold, they were blazing like fire, but not consumed. The "flames" were much like I imagine the "radiating-burning" aspect of what Moses saw when he encountered the Burning Bush on the mountainside. These seraphic forms were like that of humans; only these creatures were gigantic.

Then I heard a mighty voice that seemed to come from all directions at once, directing the seraphim, "Lower your wings." And immediately came the revelation that when we come before the Lord of the universe, He desires we cease from all other activity. We are to behold Him in all His glory, being still before His majesty, without distraction. This principle is essential for a relationship with our Holy God—and one of the most difficult to maintain.

I was struck by the radiance emanating from this heavenly place, so rich and vibrant, pulsating hues of blues, reds, and shimmering white. The color ranges are beyond description, completely defying the natural spectrum of what can be seen this side of heaven. There is simply no earthly palette that compares. It was like trying to look directly into the sun. I had to turn away because of the magnificence of His glory.

It was then that one of the seraphim flew up to me, approaching me face to face, eye to eye. I remember thinking, *He knows who I am!* The seraph paused and peered deeply into my soul. His eyes searched mine, and I instinctively knew that he was examining me, that he was reading my personal mail. Then, with a live coal he had taken with tongs from the altar, he touched my mouth and said, "See, your lips have been touched; your guilt has been taken away, and your sin atoned for"—just as he had told Isaiah.

In that moment I understood that this was, indeed, the very same seraph that had brought that flaming, purifying ember to

Isaiah's lips (see Isaiah 6:6-10). No one is permitted to remain in the Holy One's presence unless they are purified.

I found myself breathless in the presence of such glory, yet more contented and peaceful than I had ever been. This is where I had longed to be—in the presence of my heavenly Father.

"How magnificent!" I murmured over and over, exclaiming over His incomprehensible beauty.

But it was not intended that I should remain. I was to return to earth and share this message: *Heaven is available to all—not just to some, but to all who know Yeshua as Lord and Savior and who earnestly hunger and thirst for His presence.*

How glorious real righteousness looks when shrouds of preoccupation, the concerns of the world, and all manner of other earthly flotsam are forgotten as we connect with the One with whom we were created to fellowship forever.

Centennial Medical Center

The very next day I was admitted to the Emergency Room of Nashville's Centennial Medical Center with a raging fever. My heart rate was galloping along in excess of 125 beats per minute. Lisa signed consent forms permitting a slew of tests, including a spinal tap.

The room, with its glaring lights and sterile impersonal medical equipment, was bustling with activity. The doctors and nurses scurried about, carrying out their respective duties. The results of the spinal tap were ominous: white blood cells had invaded my spinal fluid. There are not supposed to be any white blood cells in spinal fluid at all, yet there were 14,900+ per cc. My platelet count was below 67,000 per cc of blood (a condition known as thrombocytopenia) instead of the normal range of 350,000 to 400,000.

Doctors barraged Lisa with questions regarding my recent activities: Where had I been? Whom had I been with? What had I eaten and where did I eat it? Had I ever had tick bites? Had I traveled recently outside the country? Doctors suspected some form of meningitis, tick-borne illness, Rocky Mountain fever, E. coli, or some other serious condition. It was surreal, like a scene from a movie.

At first, Lisa and Georgia were told I had the worst form of meningitis—meningococcal—and would have to be quarantined. In addition, Lisa and Georgia would also have to be quarantined, and they were instructed to list everyone with whom they had been in contact. Lisa had to call my boss at the dealership to drop that bomb, as it could affect the health and lives of both clients and employees. Even more alarming, Georgia, the director of a preschool, was in contact with many children daily. Every person that had been in touch with us would need to be notified, with the possibility of an extensive quarantine. Medical personnel sealed the room immediately, and threw a couple packages of protective clothing—gown, mask, and gloves—at Lisa and Georgia. The prospects were staggering, a real nightmare.

I was then transferred to the ICU. There, the doctor in charge told Lisa that my kidneys and liver were failing. It was the next morning before Lisa was informed that the meningitis diagnosis was incorrect. As the doctors continued receiving updated test results and additional information, I was finally diagnosed with MSSA: methicillin-sensitive staphylococcus aureus, an infection that was the primary causal agent for most of the symptoms.

Lisa: *I was so overwhelmed with all the medical jargon that I could not really grasp everything I was being told. I was informed* that Hugh's blue Camelbak water bottle and favorite jeans would have to be destroyed because of the contagion risk, but I insisted on taking home his favorite jeans.

A compassionate nurse, Brenda, calmly introduced me to the ICU. This was another God-incident; she was perfectly appointed by the Lord, guiding me through the procedures necessary for ICU protocol and sanitation. Anyone coming into the room had to put on masks and gloves, which then had to be immediately removed when exiting. I even slept with them on me. This was very surreal for me. I felt it was a scene from a Contagion-style movie. Nonetheless, I was not fearful or worried, in the midst of this whirlwind God had covered me with His supernatural peace. It was truly a peace that surpassed all understanding. I had an incredible assurance that God wasn't giving me more than I could handle.

Although faced with a really bad report from the doctors—my husband's possible death—I knew I was being sustained in the Lord's embrace. During the days to come, those who knew me well commented on my remarkably calm demeanor. They did not understand that it wasn't me at all, but God in me that accomplished this. I take no credit for this tremendous outpouring of amazing grace. He comes in, intervening and sustaining, if you allow Him to. I honestly don't know how people can live without Yeshua. He is the only One who can calm every storm.

The attending physician told me: "If this were my spouse or one of my family members, I would not leave him tonight." It was his way of telling me that there was a strong possibility Hugh might not survive the night. But I knew that he would live and not die; I knew that God was not finished with him yet. At that time, God hadn't revealed to me the reason I was given such a supernatural confidence. Later on, I realized I had peace because Hugh had been given a message to carry back.

A Kiss From God

I was incoherent for the first couple of days, experiencing what is referred to in medical terms as AMS, "altered mental state." I was unable to recognize my wife or anybody else, but I became extremely agitated when Lisa wasn't there. Over the course of a couple days, I had pulled all the IVs out twice, splattering blood everywhere. At this point a decision was made to put restraining gloves on me and bind my arms to prevent me from harming myself.

I was like an Alzheimer's patient, asking the same questions every ten to fifteen minutes. This was due to the septic emboli (a type of infection with bacteria, resulting in the formation of pus) affecting my brain, also causing me to one day speak with a British accent; on another, to sing a medley of songs from the '50s to the '80s. In the midst of the seriousness of it all, Lisa felt the humor was a "kiss from God," a pleasant distraction.

At this time I was in acute liver and renal failure. On August 2, some of our friends got together to pray, interceding for my healing. Our friend Harriett started praying specifically for a miracle: for a total reversal of the kidney and liver failure. The next day Dr. Mehta delivered great news, announcing in his own words that we had seen a miracle! Incredibly, my kidney and liver function had been restored to normalcy overnight!

Lisa: *My response to the doctor's wonderful news was: "THANK YOU, YESHUA!" Up until this point, his was the only positive news, and yet I remained totally confident, knowing that God "had this."*

Although there were intercessors all over the world lifting Hugh up, none of my closest friends and family who were there at the hospital with me thought Hugh would survive. They were all saying positive words to encourage and support me, but their body language told me differently. I felt it was just Yeshua and I.

Frankly, I wondered how anyone living through a situation like this could cope. Some might say that I was in denial, and yet I knew my husband would not only survive, but thrive and fulfill his God-appointed destiny.

Heart-sick

But the battle was far from over. Soon after the recorded miracle of my restored kidneys and liver, cardiologist Dr. Thomas McRae was brought in to examine me. Upon looking at the palms of my hands and soles of my feet, he noticed many red, raised lesions, which he immediately and correctly diagnosed as Janeway's lesions, aka Osler's nodes. I later told Lisa that those stigmata-like symptoms were given to me to remind me of how much pain my Messiah had suffered for me, for all of us.

It turns out they are uniquely associated with infective endocarditis, a type of infection, an inflammation of the inner lining of the heart, the endocardium. My heart rate was fast and irregular, signaling atrial fibrillation. Further tests revealed that the mitral valve, one of four valves in the heart, had been severely damaged by the infection, and blood flow was regurgitating inside my heart.

I had also developed respiratory problems, and pneumonia had set in. My breathing had become quite labored and rapid; it was painful for me to draw a breath. Respiratory therapists administered treatments through a breathing mask, but my breathing had become so difficult I had to arch my back just to be able to take a breath. I told Lisa I was in so much pain I couldn't handle another day of this. Later, I would come to realize that it was this exact position our Lord had to take when he was nailed to the cross. Every breath must have been excruciating.

It was at this point the doctors were considering placing me in an induced coma on a ventilator so that my heart could rest.

Lisa: *That night the Hernandezes took over for me at the hospital so I could get a good night's sleep. I walked into my house and, as I crossed the threshold and closed the door, I started to release my anger at Satan. I screamed, yelled, and stomped my feet on the floor as I declared life over Hugh. I cried as I prayed, the raw emotion pouring out. I really let the devil have it!*

I'm a prayer warrior and believe strongly in the effectual prayers of the saints. But honestly there were days when I had to conserve my strength and stamina to be able to last through the long days and nights ahead of me at the hospital with my sick husband. From time to time, I prayed in the Spirit, according to Romans 8:26: "Likewise the Spirit also helps us in our weaknesses." I never before understood exactly what it meant to be carried by the prayers of the saints. But at this most difficult time, I really felt and relied on those very prayers.

My spirit compelled me to get the request out to as many people as possible through prayer chains and other venues. It is amazing that these prayer requests went out on the Internet in the twinkling of an eye and were picked up and responded to so quickly by so many. I knew that there were many people, several thousand, in fact, around the world praying and waging spiritual warfare on Hugh's behalf. I'd like to say that you should never underestimate the power of prayers directed by the Spirit of God.

> *The effectual and fervent prayers of a righteous man avails much.*
> *~ James 5:16b*

The power of prayer is so strong that we don't need to fear or give the enemy any credit for having any power over God. To think that Satan has more power than Yeshua is ridiculous. The Scriptures tell us that God inclines His ear toward us and listens, and moves at the sound of our voices. God is King of Kings, Lord over the whole Universe, Jehovah Rophe (God, my Physician). We trust in and serve the Lord God. He is sovereign and there is no one with more authority. His is the ultimate victory.

> *Praying always with all prayer and supplication in the Spirit,*
> *being watchful to this end*
> *with all perseverance and supplication*
> *for all the saints.*
> ~ Ephesians 6:18

Hello or Goodbye?

Dr. Drinkwater, a gifted cardiothoracic surgeon, was called in and the determination was made that open-heart surgery to replace my mitral valve was necessary.

My heart surgery was scheduled for August 7, eight days after being admitted. There was spirited disagreement between consulting doctors as to whether to operate or not, considering my precarious and critical state. The cardiologist, Dr. McRae, and Dr. Hester, the infectious disease specialist, felt very strongly about moving forward with the surgery, but the surgeon wanted to wait until the antibiotics had a chance to combat the systemic infection. There would be a heart catheterization on August 5 to provide a close-up of the situation. The surgery would last a few hours, and I had opted for a mechanical mitral valve made of titanium rather than an organic bovine/porcine valve to replace my damaged one. The 33mm valve from St. Jude Medical should last a lifetime, but would require my being on a blood thinner medication like Warfarin, for life.

The doctors informed Lisa that due to the large number of complications, this normally routine surgery had become high-risk. The situation had become so urgent that the team of doctors decided to move up the surgery a day earlier, unless an emergency arose and caused me to be rushed into immediate surgery.

It was at this time that our wonderful infectious disease specialist, Dr. Sydney Hester, suggested to Lisa to make the call to family and friends in case I did not survive.

My sisters, Garen and Jodi, and my daughters, Lauren and Peri, my wife's family (mother-in-law Irene, father-in-law Mel, and brother-in-law Jeff) flew in immediately, given the uncertainty of my chances of survival.

My eight-year-old daughter, Elli, had special permission to see me, possibly to say a last goodbye, as I went through this ordeal. I was surprised at the great number of friends and family that had gathered at the hospital during my stay. I thought they had made the journey, some even traveling from other states, just to say hello, but in reality, they had come to say goodbye. There were times that I had limited awareness of the things taking place, but I knew that I was hovering between two worlds, between heaven and earth.

Heaven's Portals

I am convinced that what doctors often deem hallucinations are actually visions, momentary open doors, portals created by God Himself. I had a couple experiences, which were not hallucinogenic, but rather visions given to me by the Lord.

In one of them, I saw a gigantic "man" standing in my room. He was very dark-skinned and about nine feet tall. Clearly, he was not a man at all, but, in fact, an angel. I asked Lisa if she saw him, but of course she didn't understand me as I was speaking in the Hebrew language most of the day of his appearance. Naturally, the doctors attributed that to the staph infection.

On another day, I saw a map of the city of Jerusalem on the left wall in my room. On the adjacent wall to the right, the entirety was covered with streaming financial data, like tickertape, the text of which was the color of a yellow highlighter. Whenever I focused on a particular item in the data stream, the numbers would pause momentarily and then continue. For nearly nineteen months, I had no idea regarding the connection between these two images, but the Lord showed me recently that they are, in fact, connected: His plans for blessing Jerusalem and Israel, and the negative consequences and downfall of Wall Street and global financial markets as the U.S. and the nations align themselves against her.

> "It shall happen in that day that I will make Jerusalem
> a very heavy stone for all peoples;
> all who would heave it away will surely be cut in pieces,
> though all nations of the earth are gathered against it," says the
> Lord. . . .
>
> In that day the Lord will defend the inhabitants of Jerusalem;
> the one who is feeble among them in that day shall be like David,
> and the house of David shall be like God,
> like the Angel of the Lord before them.
> It shall be in that day I will seek to destroy all the nations
> that come against Jerusalem.
> ~ Zechariah 12: 2-9

Glory Revealed

In the months preceding my illness, I had been asking God to give me more time with my family. The work days at car dealerships can be long and arduous, not leaving but a couple hours to devote to my wife and children, much less anything else. My prayers were answered in a most unusual and unexpected way.

*Dear friends, do not be surprised at the
painful trials you are suffering, as though something strange
were happening to you, but rejoice that you participate
in the sufferings of Christ, so that you may be overjoyed
when His glory is revealed.*
~ 1 Peter 4:12-13

I never really saw this illness as a terrible event. The reason? Because His glory was revealed to me as I lay close to death. Suffering like this could make a person just curl up and cry out, "Why is this happening, God?" Some might even doubt the very existence of a sovereign God. How could He allow something like this? However, through this ordeal, the Lord's presence was tangible and vibrant. I had been in the throne room and seen His glory. And I have lived to talk about it. I was allowed a glimpse of what is taking place even at this moment before God's throne, and I haven't been the same since.

* * *

I was operated on, as scheduled, on August 6. During the surgery, Lisa was notified by OR staff regarding my progress. At the conclusion of the surgery, the surgeon made an incision and placed a large drainage tube into my abdomen/diaphragm that shunted plasma and blood away from my heart, into a large, translucent portable reservoir.

Recalling this event, I am reminded of this Scripture:

> *When they came to [Yeshua] and saw that He was already dead, they did not break His legs. But one of the soldiers pierced His side with a spear, and immediately blood and water came out.*
> ~ John 19:34-35

I thanked God for choosing my particular doctors, for giving them wisdom, insight, and the necessary skill, and for His grace and mercy in carrying me through a successful surgery.

Lisa was praying that God would give her strength, bracing her for my appearance, post-surgery. The nurses had warned her that I might be bloated from fluid retention/edema, that my skin might have a ghastly pallor, and there would be intubation hoses, tubes, and wires. However, when she and our daughter Peri saw me, they were shocked at my great color and overall excellent appearance. Lisa commented that I appeared tanned, like I'd had been sunning on some tropical beach! Perhaps I had. I was Son-tanned!

* * *

The doctors told Lisa that the length of a hospital stay for a "normal" open-heart patient was five days. Because my case was unusually complicated, my recovery and rehabilitation were expected to take longer. To the astonishment of the doctors, I was taken off the ventilator, extubated, and transferred to a regular cardiac suite the next day! And when Lisa came to see me, she was shocked to find me up and out of the bed, walking down the hall with my sisters!

Although I was not out of the woods—the staph infection proved to be very stubborn, and the blood cultures kept coming back positive for the MSSA strain infection that I was fighting—I rallied and, five months later, was released from Rehab.

I didn't know at the time, but the blood clots and septic emboli in my brain from the staph infection impacted areas of my brain and memory. To this day, the total impact remains unknown.

There are other ongoing issues I must deal with as well: a condition known as expressive aphasia affecting my ability to speak fluently, significant hearing loss, and vertigo. I am no longer able to perform certain chores such as yard work, nor support my family in the manner to which we had become accustomed. But I am grateful that God has shown up supernaturally and continually in every way—often through dear friends who have brought meals, helped us pay bills, and prayed for us—meeting me right where I am.

I've finally learned what is really important. Life is not about accumulating wealth, acquiring more material goods, houses, or cars. None of those things brings lasting happiness. I don't know what tomorrow holds, but I know I can trust my faithful God—who holds tomorrow.

-11-

This Year in Jerusalem

*When the Lord brought back the captivity of Zion,
We were like those who dream.*

~ Psalm 126:1

As I moved forward toward publishing this book, we began to feel a familiar tug on our hearts. It started with Lisa; she's the dreamer, the one who can see past impossibilities.

"What if God told you that it's time to return to Israel, to Jerusalem?" she asked one day.

"Not happening!" I said. "How in the world do you think that would, or could happen?

Did you forget about . . ." And I listed a litany of "why-nots" that would have discouraged the most ardent advocate of change.

I was thinking with a small mind. Limiting my faith to what I could do. Placing boundaries around the boundless *Melech Ha Olam*, the King of the Universe. I was overwhelmed by the tremendous logistical challenges of selling our home and all that moving a family 6500 miles away entails. I questioned the marketability of our double-wide mobile home—a very nice one, but a double-wide nonetheless. Just three years earlier, we'd been told we were $30,000 "under water," owing that much more than the home and land were worth.

I also struggled with a sense of shame and failure—this mobile home was a reminder of the home we never built. In fact, not too long ago, I had secretly envied some of our much younger friends who were living in much nicer, "real" houses.

Lisa, in spite of her desire to return to Israel, was also plagued by memories regarding the challenges of adjusting to life in a foreign culture and the spiritual battles previously waged there. But I had to admit that I was being drawn back; this ancient place was pulling on my heartstrings. Deep inside myself, I knew the time would come when I would no longer be able to dismiss or resist the beckoning of the *Ruach HaKodesh*.

I just didn't see it as being anytime soon.

A Sure Sign

That would begin to change when a short time later, Elli and I came upon a swastika, three feet in diameter, spray-painted in the middle of our country road just a few hundred feet from our home. We were the only Jewish people living on our street, or anywhere within miles of there, for that matter.

Earlier, Lisa had continued to badger me: "So, let me ask you again: What will it take for you to move back?"

"A swastika would have to be painted on our house!"

Close enough, Lord! I thought. *You've caught my attention.* But inside I knew—this event was a wake-up call. I was not fearful, but in my mind's eye, I saw the plight of the Jewish people in Germany in the 1930s; most of them, distracted by other obligations, missed the significance of the swastika. Wiser heads took note of the warning, packed up their belongings, and left the country while they still could.

We continued to pray and heard once again the words of the prophets calling out to us, reminding us to pay attention to the signs. In spite of the difficulties of leaving most of what we knew, we determined not to be anxious, but to follow Him, no matter what. We were being drawn, and, yes, to a certain degree— pushed.

Better to Obey

During the time that Lisa and I began to really think about returning to Israel, we heard a profound story at our congregation, a story about a horse and the meaning of obedience and stewardship. A well-known Christian leader from Toronto, Carol Arnott, had told this story originally. As horse-lover, Carol was visiting a farm that raised Arabians. As she was given a tour, she came across a newborn colt that could not stand up.

"The colt's kneecaps are inverted," the owner told her. "Unfortunately, this is not a treatable condition. This little guy is scheduled to be put down by the end of the day."

But Carol felt led to pray over the horse. As she did, the colt was miraculously healed, and the grateful owner offered to give the colt to Carol. In Toronto where she lived, there were no stables, so it seemed impossible. Without consulting God about the matter, she declined the offer and returned to Canada the next day.

A few months later she made another trip to the horse farm, eager to see the little colt that had been miraculously healed. When she learned that the horse had been killed in a fluke lightning strike, she was shocked and grieved. When she was alone again, she cried out to God: "Why did this happen?" The Lord told her, *Because you were disobedient and refused to take stewardship over this gift, I took it back. This wouldn't have happened had you responded rightly to My instruction and prompting.*

The message was clear: We had been given divine direction, and God was asking us to obey and steward His plan for us in HaAretz (the Land). But when?

Secret Garden

Although we were now certain that we were to return to Israel, strangely enough, Lisa now heard the Lord telling us to plant a garden on our property. As she shared this with me, I paid attention. It wasn't the first time she'd heard from God about something He wanted us to do, of course.

Being "city folk," we had no grid for gardening. We had no idea what to plant or when, whether to plant from seed or to buy seedlings, how to till soil or prepare a site; we felt very much like Mr. and Mrs. Douglas from the 1960s TV comedy, *Green Acres*.

After vacillating for two months, we decided to move forward with no further understanding of the purpose of this project. Having agreed to use our front flower beds as the location, we planted tomatoes, peppers, squash, and eggplant. We fertilized and fretted, weeded and watered and, to our surprise, our little garden flourished, producing an abundant harvest!

It was after this project had been completed that God told Lisa His secret—His reason for tending this garden: *Because you have been obedient in this small thing, I will now make a way for you to return to Israel.*

The Land, the Promise

With that, feeling released to make the move to Israel, we put our house on the market, selling in less than six weeks, while many other "nicer" conventional homes remained unsold. One piece of this puzzle after another fell into place, one obstacle after another toppling like Goliath before David. While the closing was not without drama and hurdles, we finally wrapped up the sale. We packed our shipment of clothing and household goods, and moved out of our "summer cottage—the only home our eleven-year-old daughter Elli had ever really known—after nine years, two months and twelve days. Once again, we prepared to return to the Promised Land.

Recently, I have been noticing pregnant women everywhere. I felt that this was also a sign, so I asked Abba Father: "What is the meaning of this sign?"

The answer came quickly: *This season that you are moving into is pregnant with promise. You are transitioning, and just as the transition is painful for a woman in labor, the pain and travail of your transition will give way to the joy that comes after. Great things are about to be birthed. Push through. Persevere. Endure.*

Hope of Heaven

I have often wondered what my life would have been like if my choices had been different.

What if I had chosen to remain in Florida?

What if I had retained my lucrative position as a nationally-ranked Mazda salesman, continuing my quest to accumulate things I thought might heal my heart?

What if there were a way to have a "re-do" with my parents, if there were some way to go back in time and relive a better relationship with my mother and father?

Or if I had chosen George Washington University instead of FSU and become a big-shot doctor…

The Bible says, "A man makes his own plans, but God determines his steps."

I know with certainty that if I had stayed at Mazda, I would not be married today. My secretive ways and then hardened heart would have taken me further and further away from life than I had been before knowing life's Author.

If my parents and I had had a better relationship, then perhaps I could have been spared a great deal of heartache and the sinful habits that resulted. God doesn't intend for any child to go through the pain of rejection from his/her own parents. I know that, for many people, such deep foundational wounds grow into lifelong dysfunctions that ultimately wreck relationships and lives. Only God, our *heavenly* Father, can heal such wounds, and I thank Him that through Yeshua, I have been healed from the inside out.

And if I had gone to George Washington University, I would never have fathered, never have met my beautiful, firstborn daughter, Lauren. Perhaps I would have ended up a wealthy doctor treating patients like myself, but even a great doctor can't heal his own heart; only the Great Physician—God—can do that. Like gasoline on a fire, I'm certain that kind of lifestyle would have eventually consumed me, as well as many others in my path.

So, as I take a look back at my past and consider where I am presently, I can surmise two certainties:

For this Jew, death has always chased after me.
Only through Yeshua can I die to my old self and truly live.
For our light affliction, which is but for a moment,
is working for us a far more exceeding and eternal weight of glory.
~ 2 Corinthians 4:17

Are You a Gambler?

"…but you MUST wager. It is not optional. You are embarked.
Which will you choose then; let us see…."

~ Blaise Pascal, Pensees, 1660

The battle between faith (heart and spirit) and reason (logic and natural intelligence) is an ancient one. Pascal points out that the "wager" has been set, whether you have thought about eternity or not. As an atheist, my denial of God didn't make the existence of heaven or hell any less real, any more than not being able to see gravity means that it is nonexistent.

By receiving the free gift given by God to us and for us and embarking on our own journey into Light and Life, we wager not. God, heaven and hell are all very real. Not only do we have the assurance of spending all eternity in His presence, but we get to enjoy all the benefits of God's many promises in this life:

"For I know the plans I have for you," says the Lord,
"plans to prosper you and not to harm you,
plans for your hope and a future."
~ Jeremiah 29:11

Yes, it's still a wild journey with high points and lows, but God promises to be with us, never to leave us or forsake us.

Never. So what happens after death, after the last breath leaves our bodies? Since my "bet" is that God is real—and remember, I have seen heaven—I believe... *I know*... that I will be instantly with the Lord.

But, you argue, what if there is no God, what if the billion-plus believers in Yeshua are wrong? When they die, closing their eyes for the last time, there is a 50 percent possibility that there is simply nothing. My answer? If so, at least, we will have lived good lives, loved well, and blessed those we have touched.

On the other hand, what if you're wrong? What if it is all true? Almighty God, Yeshua's atoning sacrifice, heaven, hell—all of it? The Wager is 50/50, and you are, as Pascal stated, "embarked." You have placed your bet. There is only one choice that makes sense. So I encourage you, I plead with you, to receive the greatest Gift ever offered mankind, and don't delay! Today could be the last day of your (physical) life.

My friend, if you have come this far with me on my journey, please heed my warning. Listen to this "dead" Jew talking. Salvation... don't leave earth without it!

Appendix

Later, when I was finally discharged from my hospital stay, I could barely comprehend the terms in my medical file. The Bible refers to these ailments that attack our mortal bodies as "light and momentary afflictions." At the time, the afflictions seemed neither light nor momentary.

Diagnoses:

1. Endocarditis with methicillin-sensitive staphylococcus aureus
2. Atrial fibrillation
3. Altered mental state
4. Bacterial meningitis
5. Tick-borne fever
6. Acute renal failure
7. Thrombocytopenia
8. Mitral Valve Disease
9. Post-operative orthostatic hypotension
10. Septic emboli and small brain abscess in occipital lobe
11. Anxiety
12. Pleural effusions
13. Visual changes with visual floaters
14. Hearing impairment/Inner ear damage in left ear

I was shocked that this illness could happen to me, shocked at what my body had suffered. I had been afflicted by a maelstrom of maladies, and was astonished that I had survived. Somehow—with God's help, the prayers of His people, and the wisdom of the doctors and staff—I had been preserved, though just barely hanging onto the fragile thread we call "life."

I had always been healthy and had taken my robust condition for granted, especially considering my age. I arrogantly thought I would always be healthy. I had even quipped to Lisa and some close friends just a few months earlier, "I'll only be going into a hospital one time . . . but when I do, it'll be a doozie."

Was this a foolish self-fulfilling prophecy?

I have since learned to be careful of the words I proclaim: "*Death and life are in the power of the tongue*" (Proverbs 18:21a). There is "someone" out there who is prowling around, overhearing your careless talk, and just waiting to take you up on it!

Cardiologic Summary and Physician's Impression:

In August 2012, Mr. Hugh Nemets developed Bacterial Endocarditis. This is an infection in which bacteria adheres to the surface of a heart valve and begins to eat away at the valve tissue. As the infection continues, parts of the infectious growth can break off, enter the blood stream and spread throughout the body, setting up infections or abscesses in other organs.

If left untreated, Bacterial Endocarditis is universally fatal. Even with intensive care and modern treatment of antibiotics and surgery, the death rate is high.

Mr. Nemets's case was demarcated with many poor prognostic signs. In the first few days of his hospital stay, the evidence of the seriousness and complications of his infection would have indicated he might not survive.

It looked like he needed a miracle.

Mr. Nemets's symptoms began with a headache, fever and muscular pain. He was examined at a local emergency room and given initial medical treatment and sent home. At home, his condition deteriorated rapidly as he developed high fevers, back pain, and mental confusion. He was admitted to one of Nashville's major medical centers for evaluation. He had initial testing including blood tests, X-rays, an abdominal ultrasound, and a spinal tap. There was evidence of an infection with elevated blood cell counts, and abnormal spinal fluid with his initial diagnosis as possible meningitis. Abnormal blood tests also noted kidney failure, liver failure and sepsis--a bacterial infection in the blood. Mr. Nemets was immediately placed on a regimen of high-powered antibiotics for treatment. The doctors ordered an Echocardiogram, an ultrasound of the heart, looking for the source of the infection. The echocardiogram revealed a deformity of the mitral valve of the heart called mitral valve prolapse; the main pump chamber of the heart called the ventricle was extremely weak. This finding prompted the physicians to search further with a trans-esophageal echocardiogram. This is an ultrasound performed with a probe down the esophagus, which is better able to investigate the mitral valve. The test revealed the infection. It was a large growth of bacteria on the mitral valve of the heart, and it was eating away the tissue of the valve and causing it to leak severely. This was causing the heart to weaken. The particular large size of the growth and the bacteria, which was called staph aureus, were both poor prognostic findings.

The diagnosis was made: Bacterial Endocarditis. The treatment with antibiotics had already been initiated. Despite 72 hours of treatment, Mr. Nemets was getting worse. He developed memory deficits; visual disturbances and hearing loss; a Brain MRI scan showed the infection had spread to his brain, eyes and the inner ear. In addition, he developed breathing difficulty, respiratory distress with a CT scan showing fluid around his heart and in his lungs. He was in congestive heart failure, a serious complication, and the result of the further deterioration of the heart valve with the weakened heart muscle and fluid was backing up in the lungs.

He also developed a rhythm abnormality that further impaired the heart's ability to pump properly. The doctors had to decide about open-heart surgery to replace his failing valve. This type of surgery, in the setting of an active infection and a very weakened heart muscle, was very high risk; he might not survive the operation. On the other hand, he was not responding to the standard antibiotic treatment and, if the valve was not fixed, he would likely die of heart failure within days.

The decision was made. The high-risk surgery was his only chance. On August 6, 2012, he was taken to the operating room where he was placed on the bypass machine. His heart was stopped and the infected incompetent valve tissue was cut out of his heart and a new mechanical valve was sewn into place. The heart was then closed up and restarted on its own as warm blood began to circulate through the reconstructed heart.

Post-operatively, Hugh was still not out of danger and required high-powered antibiotics to treat the areas where the infection had spread including his brain, eyes and ears. The infection had to be completely eradicated and would require weeks of treatment. He also required intensive care and support to clear the fluids out of his lungs, and to optimize the chance of recovery of his kidneys and liver and brain function. After a month of hospitalization, he was discharged and continued to receive antibiotics at home. He recovered full heart function and his valve is working well. He continues to suffer with hearing loss and memory lapses that were a consequence of the brain infection.

In summary, the severity of Mr. Nemets's poor prognostic indicators and the severity of his illness raised significant doubts for his survival in the minds of his physicians.

Apparently, God has further plans for his life.

Rick L. Bennett, M.D., FACC
Division Head, Cardiovascular Services
St. Thomas West Hospital, Nashville, TN